Whose Future
Are You Financing?

What the Government and Wall Street
Don't Want You To Know

Whose Future Are You Financing?

What the Government and Wall Street Don't Want You To Know

If what you *thought* to be true turned out not to be,

when would you want to know about it?

David Lukas

DLShowOnline.com
InfiniteFinancialServices.com

1-800-559-0933

This book is for educational purposes with the sole intent to educate the reader on its subject matter. By writing this book, the author is not giving legal, tax or investment advice. The author does not have any knowledge of the reader's specific financial situation; therefore readers should consult a professional before acting on any of the information contained in this book. Because each individual's situation is different, specific advice should be tailored to the particular circumstances. For this reason, the reader is advised to consult with his or her own advisor regarding that individual's specific situation. The author has taken reasonable precautions in the writing of this book and believes the facts presented in the book are accurate as of the date it was written. However, the author specifically disclaims any liability resulting from the use or application of the information in this book. The information in this book is not intended to serve as legal advice related to individual situations. If you need legal advice or other professional assistance, you should seek the services of a competent professional.

To obtain more copies of this book please visit www.InfiniteFinancialServices.com.

ISBN # 978-0-9883878-3-6

What others are saying about this book

"There is an overwhelming need for sound financial advice in today's financial economy. David has brilliantly explained why the traditional banking methods have failed time and time again and what you can do to create your own wealth. WHOSE FUTURE ARE YOU FINANCING will dramatically change your view of what you thought to be true for so long.

Unfortunately, common knowledge of banking and finance is just the tip of the iceberg. It's the part under the surface of the water that causes the most damage. This book exposes the iceberg under the surface waiting to sink your financial retirement ship."

Seth Wilson, D.C. Chiropractic Physician
Arkansas Center for Physical Medicine and
Rehabilitation, North Little Rock, AR

"Amschel Rothschild said, "Give me control of a nation's money, and I care not who makes its laws." We live in a country that uses a rigged monetary system, and there is no way to "win" when we play by their rules. David's book gives those of us on Main Street a powerful and life-changing alternative to Wall Street's financial plan. David's concise yet highly informative description of the Personal Monetary System is a MUST READ!!"

Reagan Baber, MD
Chandler Advisors, LLC--Director of Economics

"David has done a masterful job of exposing financial concepts anyone can implement into their financial strategies. The principles are easy to understand and provide a great path for wealth creation. This book is a "must have" for anyone who wants to improve their financial position."

Deron K. Hamilton, CPA
Partner - Denman, Hamilton, & Associates CPA PLLC

"David's research and insight about Banking, Finance, Wall Street and the insurance industry is a must for the critical thinker and investor. Reading David's book will open your eyes and help you take control of your finances by resurrecting the truth. Don't be surprised if you tune out all that prime time financial noise and cancel that money publication. David's book is a must read!"

John M. Little IV
Income Planning Specialist
JML Financial

"As a mortgage expert, I spend the majority of my time educating clients on the proper way to manage their mortgage. David has done an excellent job of challenging conventional wisdom when it comes to the subject of mortgages. After reading WHOSE FUTURE ARE YOU FINANCING, you will realize that much of what you have been taught about mortgages simply isn't true. You will never look at your mortgage the same way again."

Lee Welfel
Mortgage Originator
Author of *The Mortgage Book*

"This book will challenge your belief system about money and wealth creation. These ideas and strategies are uncommon and are not taught through traditional education. David does an excellent job of presenting the FACTS and sharing the TRUTH about how money works. Prepare to be enlightened if you are serious about your financial future."

Matt Haas, MBA
Business Owner and IFS Client

"This book will expose the highly 'abstract by design' methods and financial products the Government and Wall Street implement to separate you from your hard earned money. David's book will show you simple ways to begin securely financing your own future and limit the personal wealth you transfer away from fees and taxes."

Michael Massucco
Personal Investor and IFS Client

"David Lukas is passionate about his work and the service he provides his clients. His knowledge and understanding of mortgage and financial products puts David in a position to analyze situations from a "big picture" perspective. He shares valuable insight and critical information with readers as he provides Simple Strategies to maximize your finances and your future. Packed with "harsh realities" that everyone deserves to know, WHOSE FUTURE ARE YOU FINANCING is a must read for everyone."

Steven Blackwood, CDPE, CREE, RDCPro Certified
Distressed Property Expert Arkansas Master Broker
NRBA

"As a talk show host who has interviewed hundreds of authors over my 30+ year radio career, I understand how important it is to give facts in a concise and understanding way. Others have written multiple books in an attempt to expose the financial truths that David has successfully outlined in fewer than 150 pages. This little book in your hands is very readable. Save your time and money and read David's book!"

Dave Elswick
Host of The Dave Elswick Show KARN
Little Rock, AR

"Benjamin Franklin's phrase 'Time is Money' is considered one of the most profound quotes in finance and business. Not many people actually understand what he meant. In David's book you will get the real wisdom of this phrase and learn several ways to secure your financial future. His book brings together revolutionary ideas about finance, and is the most important step towards securing financial freedom for those who want to take the leap of faith."

Tarun Pandey, MD
Radiologist

Acknowledgements

Thank you to Leah, my beautiful wife of 14 years, for enduring my business endeavors since the early 90's. Your patience and constant support is appreciated! In truth, I have the easy job. I am grateful for the endless hours you invest in our three children, Benjamin and Audrey, and Zach. Raising kids in today's world is no small undertaking!

I am grateful to both of my parents who never gave up on me while I was in school. Thank you, Thank You, Thank You!

I am most grateful for the unconditional love and grace given to me by God through the sacrifice of His Son. Despite my many shortcomings, God continues to love and pursue me.

I am thankful for each and every day that God has given me here on planet Earth. I strive to live in today as tomorrow may not come. As a human being, it's easy to get caught up in the mindset of thinking, "When I get this new job, then I will be happy. When this happens, then I will be content." I encourage you to be thankful and live in today. Life is today! Tomorrow may never come. As the days go by, I am beginning to realize just how short life is. Even if I live to be 100, life on earth is like a vapor; you see it, and then it's gone. I strive to maintain this perspective and live my life with this in mind while being thankful for every breath that God has given me.

Thank you to John Little who has been a great friend and business partner. I appreciate the time that we have spent learning from one another.

Thank you to all of my clients and friends whom I have had the opportunity to serve. Without you, I couldn't do what I do!

Lastly, I want to acknowledge my deceased business partner and friend who taught me so much. On October 23rd, 2012, Val Wheeler died of a massive heart attack. Val was just 56. I can say that he died doing what he loved doing (literally, he was giving a presentation to a group of doctors at the time of his death). Val was a generous man who willingly gave of his time and resources. He will be missed.

Table of Contents

Foreword

A few years ago a good friend approached me proclaiming that he had found some modern day 'secret of finance.' This gentleman and I had worked together at one of the largest broker-dealers in the country just a few years earlier, before his sudden exit which left us all scratching our heads. Who knew that I would make that same sudden exit nearly a year later. At the time I was well on my way to becoming one of the top financial advisors/money managers in the southern U.S. Being that I thought I knew better, I brushed him off. But he was relentless. Finally I gave in and read a book about what David calls your _Personal Monetary System_. This system was so interesting, so exciting that I couldn't stop studying and researching it.

Finally, after a year of utter research, trying to find all the loopholes and pit falls of this little-known strategy, I came to the conclusion that this was the most effective financial management and growth system Americans have access to today—and that they've had access to for the last 200 years for that matter. Within sixty days of reaching that conclusion I left that broker-dealer and published the research I'd spend nearly twelve months building.

Over the coming months I spent my time searching for people who had heard of, or were willing to learn about, this _Personal Monetary System_. Then something remarkable happened. On a beautiful summer Saturday, one of those days that you know God created to let us know He's there, I was in the car moving through radio stations trying to find something worth listening to. Then I hear this gentleman on some talk radio station talking about the very topics I'd been researching! That gentleman was David Lukas, and he was debunking the conventional wisdom that fifteen-year mortgages saved you money compared to thirty-year mortgages. I was hooked! So I did what any sane person would do – I *Googled* his name.

What I found only hooked me more. Archives of radio shows and writings detailing the creation of the Federal Reserve, why mutual funds had robbed so many Americans blind, and why most banks put more money in insurance contracts than they do in real estate or bonds. Nearly a year after this happened I became aware that an insurance company executive whom I knew also knew David. And the rest is history, as they say.

David and I met and I realized that he had more to offer than he probably knew. For those that have acquired this book, you're in for a real blessing. Mr. Lukas has outlined for us exactly what this little-known financial system is and, almost more importantly, why most of you have never heard of it. There are great powers, powers that are many times behind the scenes, that won't benefit from our education on the topics that David writes about. What you're about to gain really cannot be described briefly. It will take you on a journey, challenge your preexisting beliefs, and lead you to a land of prosperity that you may not have known existed.

George Orwell once said, "In a time of deceit, telling the truth is a revolutionary act." The truth that is in this book isn't to be taken lightly—and it *is* revolutionary. The more you read, the more you study, the more you analyze, the more you will come to understand that what the majority are taught to do financially is inconceivably inaccurate.

2

You'll realize that many people get rich in the process— but usually you aren't one of them. By reading this book you'll get the inside scoop on how the wealthy *really* manage their money. And it will lead you to places you never thought you could go.

Let the prosperity begin!

B. Chase Chandler
Founder of Chandler Advisors
Author of *The Wealthy Family*

Challenging Paradigms

When Christopher Columbus set sail to explore The New World, everybody thought he was crazy. They said, "You're going to sail right off the end of the earth." "He's a madman." "He'll never make it back." *Whatever they may have said or thought, we know now that what the majority of people believed at that time was actually not true.* The idea that the earth was flat was so ingrained in their culture that they couldn't fathom anything different, let alone an entirely new paradigm.

When Galileo was looking through his telescope, he came to the conclusion that it was not the sun that rotated around the earth, but that the earth rotated around the sun. This totally rocked "common" logic and belief. At that time, this belief was so ingrained in the culture and society that the Catholic Church said Galileo's claim was against all things holy and even blasphemous to Scripture itself. It was heresy. Because of these long-held beliefs, they imprisoned him. We know today that indeed the earth does rotate around the sun. We know this to be true, but everyone at that time thought otherwise because that's what they had been taught to believe.

So, the point of this book is to challenge your assumptions. I want to challenge what you think you know about your personal finances. What you've learned from schools, magazines, media or Wall Street itself may not be true, and in reality is not true.

Jimmy's Dilemma

I have a client (we'll call him Jimmy) who is 72 years old. He's retiring this year and he has accumulated approximately $1.3 million in savings.

When I first met with Jimmy and we analyzed his current financial position, I quickly realized he had all of the $1.3 million dollars in equities (the stock market). That meant 100% of his life savings was at risk. If the market went through another "correction" of say 25%, Jimmy could lose more than $300,000 of his retirement savings. He couldn't afford that! He doesn't have time to regain that type of loss. As my good friend John Little says,

"There are no do-overs
when you are this close to retirement."

Wall Street uses terminology like "securities" to describe what you are buying but I would say, based on the unpredictable volatility of the market, **there is nothing secure about securities.**

Wall Street has its own terminology. When the market has a "correction", like in '08 when the S & P 500 dropped 37% affecting many retirement fund accounts, they say this is "normal" and that everything will bounce back in time – "it always has." That's not too comforting for Jimmy.

Jimmy has told me that he can't afford a market "correction." Why *do* they call it that? There is nothing "correct" about a correction! When we sat down to discuss his future he said, "I've always thought this was the only way." Jimmy, like many others I meet, has been duped into believing there's only one path to saving for retirement. Wall Street likes to call it "investing." I prefer the term gambling.

What Jimmy has now discovered is that what he's been sold all these years—that he had to put his money at risk—is not true. This "take a risk and wait it out" investment strategy has all been unnecessary. He could have achieved the same results while knowing exactly how much money he would have after retirement (isn't that what we all really want to know?), that he cannot outlive his income (what I call "income for life"), and that it would all be guaranteed to be there when he needed it (what I call Retirement Without Risk).

It still surprises me when I meet people who have lost untold amounts of money in the market, yet they continue to "feed the beast" by putting money into the market month after month. Many of them are simply hoping they will get back what they've put in.

Another story, that hits close to home, comes from a family member through marriage who told me of her own very painful experience. She inherited approximately $1 million worth of stock held in one company and at the time she was advised to keep it "invested." The name of this company was WorldCom. Need I say more? Without getting into all the details, the company emerged from bankruptcy during 2004 and the value of the stock she inherited became completely worthless. $1 million lost practically overnight. She doesn't like to talk about this story too much. It was a very painful lesson indeed.

Remember: It is equally important to get a return of your money, as it is to get a return on your money.

An investment operation is one, which upon thorough analysis, promises safety of principal and an adequate return. Operations not meeting these requirements are speculative.

- Benjamin Graham, The Intelligent Investor

Ask yourself this question:

When someone advises you to put your money at risk (by speculating in the Market), *whose* money is at risk? Yours...or theirs?

It's unfortunate that the prevalent mindset of achieving retirement savings objectives is often synonymous with taking on more risk. Risk can be defined as exposure to loss. Synonyms for risk include: to endanger, jeopardize, to gamble with, to take chances, to put on the line, to put in jeopardy. The greatest definition of Risk is the likelihood of loss.

Most people mistakenly associate risk (related to their retirement savings) with the probability that they will "hit it out of the park" or "win big" by experiencing higher rates of return. The true definition of risk is the likelihood of loss. Let's think through this logic for a moment.... You have to take on more chance of losing everything, so you can get more money and get ahead? Logically does this make sense? Yet, this is sold to the American public by most "Financial Advisers" promoting common strategies propagated by Wall Street.

Before we proceed, I would like to say that I am not inherently against having a small portion of your money at risk. Any money you decide to put at risk, ultimately, should be money you are willing to lose—money you are NOT counting on for retirement! You can achieve outstanding results without taking substantial risk. Most people who are saving for retirement have the majority of their money at risk with NO guarantees, but the good news is there is an alternative.

Outliving Your Income

Jimmy commented to me recently, "I don't necessarily have to worry about outliving my income because most of my relatives have only lived into their 70s. I'm 72...."

"Not to worry...your money line is longer than your life line."

What he's failing to realize is that he cannot plan his future based on the life span of others.

My grandmother is 98 years old and she still lives alone. Her mind is sharp, though she does have someone regularly visit to help her with some tasks. Grandma has outlived her two younger sisters and older brother. We all know that people are living longer than ever before, and my grandma is a perfect example.

Similarly, my grandfather (my mom's dad) recently turned 92 and also lives at home. I'm witnessing my parents take care of their parents like so many are doing today. I can tell you firsthand that the time and energy they're investing in the care of my grandparents is very real. Someone now must stay with my grandfather night and day. This is a reality for many, and will become more "normal" in the future. It's risky to assume, "Well, I just won't live that long so I don't need to worry about how long my income will last." We need to be wise in our planning so we're not to be a burden to our children and so that we'll be able to enjoy life and retire without risk or worry.

Something else about grandma that I think is a little funny, is that she's a bit of a hypochondriac. Over the years grandma would often say, "Oh, I just know I have cancer. I know it. This is it." And then the doctor would give her a clean bill of health. I always joke that when she's 102 she'll go to the doctor and they'll tell her, "Edna, we're sorry to tell you this but... you have cancer." And she'll reply, "I knew it all along!" Well, grandma, you have to go sometime. If you've made it to 102, every day is a bonus!

The point of these stories is that you really don't know how long you will live. That's why it's imperative to know that your retirement income is going to be there when you need it, for as long as you need it, without interruption, "correction," or risk. That is why I take a more conservative approach with an income-for-life strategy, which guarantees you won't outlive your money. This is the only method I know of that gives you both complete control and peace of mind so you can enjoy life now and Retire Without Risk.

By following this proven system (which we'll get to in a few pages), you'll know *exactly* how much money you'll have coming to you every month for the rest of your life. It's what I like to call your own Personal Private Pension – or "Mailbox Money" for short.

If you're like most of my clients, all your life you've been taught to believe that saving for retirement through the stock market is the only option. You've probably also been told not to worry about market fluctuations, to stay the course, and that over time you'll recover whatever you've lost.

Main Street has been continually seduced by the overly optimistic gambling nature of Wall Street. We've been sold on the "fact" that the only way to accumulate money is by speculating. I think it was Schoolhouse Rock® that taught us to: "Buy low, sell high, take a piece of the pie – that's the Wall Street way."

So from our earliest years as children, we've been conditioned to believe that "the Street" was the best way to save for retirement. The problem is that isn't true. There's another way.

The hope the folks living on "Main Street" have is that when they hit Jimmy's age, they will have enough money saved to have a decent income for the rest of their life. That's what we all want. We don't know exactly how much we're going to have, we just *hope* our nest egg is big enough to sustain us until we die.

Is your goal for retirement...

a) To be ultra-wealthy? Or,
b) To have income for life and maintain your standard of living?

The hope of Main Street is that Wall Street has the solution. What you're about to find out is that that's not necessarily the case.

Why Compound Interest Doesn't Work

Albert Einstein said that "compound interest is the 8th wonder of the world." It works best uninterrupted and over time. When money is put aside and left untouched to collect interest year after year, the result is nearly miraculous.

Compounding interest doesn't work for so many Americans. They fail to save any substantial amount of money during their lifetime, because they have no method to gain use and control of their money during the compounding period. Spending the money you are supposed to be saving interrupts the compounding process and "kills the miracle" that makes compound interest work.

What's the secret to this miracle you ask. . .

You **NEVER** Touch the Principal.

This allows the interest to compound continually (upon itself and the principal) so that you earn increasing amounts of growth as the years go by.

For Example: If you put just $100 a month away for 40 years, compounding at 7%, your $48,000 has turned into $265,643! But the problem is...life happens. There are all kinds of unforeseen expenses that come up throughout life—many unanticipated, such as:

- A new air conditioning unit.
- A new roof.
- Loss of job.
- Kids need braces.
- House floods.

Most people don't have a plan (nor a method) to gain access to their money while still allowing it to compound uninterrupted. That is why most people fail to accumulate substantial savings during their life.

> Remember: The "miracle" of compound interest works best uninterrupted and overtime. If you "kill" the miracle, it doesn't work!

If you consistently save $5,000 per year and you spend what you've saved in the 5th year, it would represent a long-term loss of $229,000 over your lifetime!
(See Figure 1.1)

The True Cost Of Paying Cash

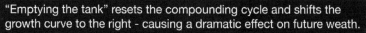

"Emptying the tank" resets the compounding cycle and shifts the growth curve to the right - causing a dramatic effect on future weath.

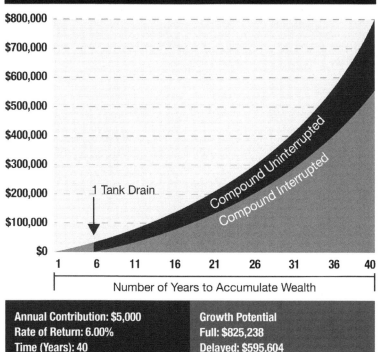

Annual Contribution: $5,000	Growth Potential
Rate of Return: 6.00%	Full: $825,238
Time (Years): 40	Delayed: $595,604
	Long-Term Difference: $-229,634

Figure 1.1   Copyright 2013 Family Money Group, LLC

That's a huge loss. But this is precisely what most people do — they remove their savings to make a purchase, thus "killing the miracle" of compound interest. Then, when they reach retirement, they don't have nearly enough saved and are putting themselves at great risk of running out of money.

The example in Figure 1.1 (page 15) assumes you only make one cash purchase in your lifetime. What about the person who pays cash for every automobile purchase? After all, isn't "paying cash" what we are taught is the wise financial choice? If a household acquires just 1 vehicle every 6 years and paid cash for a total of 7 cars over a 40 year time frame, this would represent a long term loss of $797,053! (See Figure 1.2 below)

The True Cost Of Paying Cash

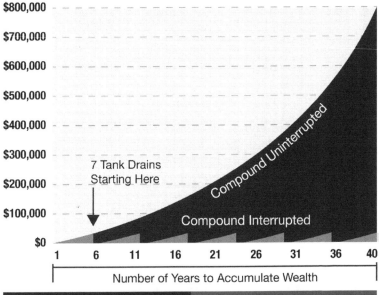

"Emptying the tank" resets the compounding cycle and shifts the growth curve to the right - causing a dramatic effect on future weath.

7 Tank Drains Starting Here

Compound Uninterrupted

Compound Interrupted

Number of Years to Accumulate Wealth

Annual Contribution: $5,000	Growth Potential
Rate of Return: 6.00%	Full: $825,238
Time (Years): 40	Delayed: $28,185
Car purchase made every 6 years	Long-Term Difference: $-797,053

Figure 1.2   Copyright 2013 Family Money Group, LLC

This is a conservative estimate as we assume that every car costs only what was accumulated before the savings were depleted ($34,877) every six years to make the auto purchase. Most likely the cost of transportation would increase over 40 years.

A better strategy is to allow your money to compound continually and have complete access to use it for purchases, while never actually touching the principal. In this way your money continues to grow, you get to buy the things you want and need, and you'll be able to retire without risk knowing exactly how much income you'll have for the rest of your life.

This isn't a "new" idea or method by any means. In fact, it's been around for over 150 years and is the primary way the wealthy families in our country pass their wealth from generation to generation.

Wall Street doesn't want you to know about this method because they want you to speculate in the stock market. The government doesn't want you to understand this because they want to tax your investments when you begin taking them out of the stock market.

The time has come for those on Main Street to wake up and consider a better method for saving money that creates guaranteed income for life so you can retire without risk. But first you need to understand the different types of money and how they affect your lifestyle now and in the future.

3 Types of Money

Would you believe that there are three types of money?

1. Accumulated
2. Lifestyle
3. Transferred

Accumulated money is what you are saving. This is where advisors, especially those who refer to having "money under management" narrowly focus. Their primary focus is on how much money you need to accumulate during your working years in order to have enough to retire and not outlive your money.

The conversation is often focused on rates of return and typically goes something like this: "You are averaging 5% currently. I think I can get you 7% if we move your money into this other product or investment vehicle." Their focus is on chasing higher rates of return. When you follow this counsel, you are typically taking unnecessary risks. They're asking the wrong question.

Note: You must understand there's a big difference between average rate of return and real rates of return. The first is a mathematical equation; the later is what you actually get to spend.

For example, If you have $100,000 invested and you experienced a 100% gain, you now have $200,000. If the following year your account goes down by 55% you end up with just $90,000. Your "average" rate of return was 22.5% (you gained 100% and and then lost 55%) But your actual real rate of return was a negative -5.13%, you lost money!

Next, there's **lifestyle** money, which everyone can identify with. Lifestyle money is simply the money you're spending today to maintain your current standard of living; the car you drive, the house you live in, how many times you eat out, the vacations you take, etc. It encompasses the money you spend, after taxes, for consuming goods and services. It's the money you live off of to maintain your standard of living—your lifestyle.

Lastly, there is what we call **transferred** money. This is money that you are typically transferring away unknowingly and unnecessarily.

> The two largest wealth transfers that take place in your life are **taxes** and the way you manage your **mortgage**. For business owners, it is the way they handle their cash flow, financing and taxes.

A dollar paid in taxes unnecessarily not only costs you that dollar, but also what that dollar could have earned you over the next 5, 10, 15, or 30 years had it been allowed to keep earning interest in your account. When you transfer money to someone else you are "killing the miracle" of compounding interest. It doesn't have to be this way.

This loss of the use of your money is known as lost opportunity cost. Most financial planners fail to take into consideration lost opportunity cost and the time value of money. What I mean by that is, simply stated:

If you have a dollar today and you transfer it to someone else, not only did you lose that dollar, but what that dollar *could have earned you* over time had you not given it away.

Lost Opportunity cost has been given little to no attention in retirement planning circles. This is unfortunate because it is very real and can cost you dearly. It is crucial that you understand opportunity cost. Once you do, it will totally transform the way you manage your cash flow and handle life's major purchases.

Always Remember:

The way you spend your money is equally as important as the act of saving your money.

Now that you know about opportunity costs, you also need to know that:

You finance everything in life that you buy.

You either *pay* interest to someone else, or you *give up* the ability to earn interest (because you have transferred your money to someone else). It's part of what I call The Banking Equation.

The Banking Equation

Every one of your financial decisions creates opportunities either for you or others. Unfortunately, it's usually the latter.

To fully understand The Banking Equation, you need to first understand where money comes from. How much do you know about that Federal Reserve note that's in your wallet?

The average person gives little to no thought of how money is created in the economy. Before you start thinking about where to put your money, it's important that you understand banking, economics, and how money works. It's absolutely critical.

I recently had the opportunity to interview G. Edward Griffin on my radio show. He wrote the book "The Creature From Jekyll Island." I highly recommend you read this book. I also encourage you to listen to my interview with Mr. Griffin by going to: DLShowOnline.com/Books*.

The book gets its title from the secret meeting that took place in November of 1910 on Jekyll Island (which is a resort island off the coast of Georgia). The book tells of the birth of the nation's third central bank, The Federal Reserve, and our nation's history as it relates to money. At that meeting were six men who represented 25% of the world's wealth at the time. Think about that for a moment. Six men.

Who were these men and what were their true objectives?

These men represented the largest banks in the United States and Europe. As these big banks were competitors, why would six men representing rival banks come together in such secrecy? The primary reason: *Competition.*

In 1910, the number of banks in the United States was growing at an exponential rate. This caused the big banks in New York to suffer a consistent decline in market share.

Another trend they wanted to reverse was rising interest rates. They desired to intervene in the free market and shift interest rates downward so consumers would favor debt over savings. It was their goal to remove all restraints of the creation of money or, as they described it, to make the money more "elastic". They wanted complete control of the nation's money supply.

Another major goal of their meeting was to formulate a plan to shift any losses *from* the big banks *to* the taxpayers, while convincing Congress their plans were to protect the public. Out of this meeting came the creation of The Federal Reserve.

In the United States, money is created and controlled by the Federal Reserve, which was formed in 1913 as a result of this secret meeting. It's a seat of power that is set aside from all others in society.

The Federal Reserve is controlled by some of the richest and most politically influential families in the world, and it has the power to create money out of thin air.

Institutions like the Federal Reserve were staunchly opposed by the designers of our Constitution and by presidents such as George Washington and Thomas Jefferson.

So it's important that you understand the principle stemming from the Federal Reserve:

Money that enters our economy is created out of nothing.

"When you or I write a check there must be sufficient funds in our account to cover the check, but when The Federal Reserve writes a check, there is no bank deposit on which that check is drawn. When The Federal Reserve writes a check, it is creating money."

- Boston Federal Reserve

This is so important to understand, so hang with me as I explain this. The Federal Reserve uses fancy terms like "open market operations" and "quantitative easing" to describe their actions, but what they are really doing is creating money out of nothing. That's right, nothing!

First, the federal government issues a Treasury note or bond. It is simply a promise to pay a specific amount of money at a certain time in the future. This debt becomes the primary driving force behind our nation's money supply. These government securities function like cash, but they don't look like cash just yet. To accomplish this, the Treasury bonds are sold to a Primary Dealer who in turn sells these government IOU's to The Federal Reserve. In order for the Fed to purchase these government debts, they simply write a Federal Reserve check to make their purchase. Where did they get the money to make their purchase? **Answer**: The money did not exist. They created the money from nothing. The Fed can't bounce a check! These government debts are now considered an asset on the Fed's books. Debt an asset? Well, the thinking is that the government has the power to confiscate all the money it wants through taxation, therefore it is considered an asset. The U.S. Treasury will now "cash" that check. Remember, there was no money to back this check, but our Government wants this money to fund their insatiable appetite for spending. This is much easier than going to the people and raising taxes.

This mysterious process is intentionally wrapped up in the banking system. They want you to think the process is too complicated to understand and for you to assume they must know what they are doing. They want you to believe their actions are for your own good. Believe me, they don't want you to know the truth! Make no mistake about it, this process is no different than our government ordering the creation of money with nothing of any value backing it. It is pure fiat currency.

What is fiat currency?

The American Heritage Dictionary defines fiat money as "paper money decreed legal tender, not backed by gold or silver." The two characteristics of fiat money therefore, are: (1) it does not represent anything of intrinsic value, and (2) it is decreed legal tender. Legal tender simply means that there is a law requiring everyone to accept the currency in commerce.

The Fed's primary means of injecting new money into the economy is through what is called "Open Market Operations". When The Fed pumps $40 billion in newly created money into the economy, they accomplish this through the purchase of U.S. Treasury securities (government debt) from a primary dealer (bond dealer). In this example, the $40 billion dollars the primary dealer received from the sale of government debt (Treasury Securities) ends up being deposited into the primary dealer's bank account. As one would expect, their bank account would be credited with the $40 billion. It is at this moment that new money enters the economy through the banking system.

The bank that was on the receiving end of the $40 billion dollar deposit now has "excess reserves" which further compounds the problem. Let me explain....

We function in what is called a "fractional reserve" banking system. This means banks are only required to keep a "fraction" of a deposit holder's money on hand. For example, if you receive a $1,000 paycheck and then deposit it in your bank down the street, your bank now has "excess reserves". Banks are only required to set aside 10% of a depositor's account balance as reserves. Since your bank only needs to keep a fraction of your $1,000 deposit on hand, it now has "excess reserves". These reserves give the bank the legal ability to make new loans totaling an additional $900 to other bank customers. Where did they get the money to lend out? I think you are beginning to see the light.

In truth, the bank making the new loan simply creates dollars out of nothing and subsequently credits the borrower $900! This means that when you deposited your $1,000 paycheck at your local bank, they now have the authority to create $900 new credit dollars with nothing more than a book entry. It is at this point, that $1,900 is now circulating. The $900 loan ultimately ends up being deposited into another bank at which point the process plays itself out over and over in the banking system. Your original $1,000 deposit ultimately creates $9,000 additional digital dollars circulating throughout the economy.

This causes a direct expansion of the currency supply, which means, ultimately, it takes more of your hard earned dollars to purchase goods and services. This process begins with the Federal Reserve, however banks also have the legal ability to create money out of nothing and it's a fact, historically this is where most of the circulating dollars spring into existence. (Since 1914 we've borrowed every dollar into existence). To top it all off, they are charging you (the borrower) interest on this money!

Read the quotes below straight from the horse's mouth. The Federal Reserve states:

"Commercial banks create checkbook money whenever they grant a loan, simply by adding new deposit dollars in accounts on their books in exchange for a borrower's IOU."

~Federal Reserve Bank of New York,
"I Bet You Thought", P. 19

"The actual process of money creation takes place primarily in banks. Banks can build up deposits by increasing loans and investments. This unique attribute to the banking system was discovered by Goldsmiths."

~Federal Reserve Bank of Chicago

*See recommended reading list on page 132

The Birth of Fractional Reserve Banking

Our currency is no longer tied to gold. In fact, if you study the history of modern banking, it all began with goldsmiths who began to store their customer's precious metal coins for a fee. As you can imagine, it would be very inconvenient to lug around large amounts of gold to make your purchases, so these early bankers began issuing certificates, or bank notes. The belief was that you could redeem your certificate at any time for a specific amount of gold. People knew these early bank notes (paper money) were "as good as gold" and began trading these for goods and services instead of the actual gold itself. Again, this was much more convenient than carrying around large quantities of actual gold coins.

Over time these early bankers realized they could get away with lending up to eighty percent or more of the gold they had on deposit to other customers. Those with gold on deposit assumed this was the banker's money, but in reality it was *their* money! How could these bankers get away with this? They reasoned that it was very unlikely that a large percentage of the gold on deposit would be withdrawn at one time. So these early bankers began to loan out the deposits of others and the concept of banking as we know it was born.

Debt, Debt, Debt

> *"There are two ways to conquer and enslave a nation. One is by the sword. The other is by debt."*
>
> *- John Adams*

Did you know that every American dollar that is in circulation today was created out of a loan from a bank? You may not have borrowed it, but someone did.

In truth, money is not created until the instant it's borrowed.

I firmly believe that the entire function of the Federal Reserve is to convert debt into money.

Do you know what would happen if all of these loans were paid off? It will never happen, but imagine with me for a moment. If ALL bank loans were paid off, including the national debt, every mortgage, every credit card balance, and all other outstanding loans, there would be no money in circulation!

Even advocates of central banking have admitted this reality. Economist John Galbraith stated,

> *"Following the civil war, the Federal Government ran a heavy surplus. However, it could not pay off it's debt (retire its securities) because to do so would mean there would be no bonds to back the national bank notes. To pay off the debt was to destroy the money supply."*

At the end of the day, essentially every dollar that is in existence, including that Federal Reserve note that is in your wallet (AKA "dollar bill") or the digital money in your bank account, every dollar that you have in your possession and every American dollar circulating throughout the world, is earning *compounding interest* by the banks that created them!

> *"The few who understand the system will either be so interested in its profits or be so dependent upon its favors that there will be no opposition from that class, while on the other hand, the great body of people, mentally incapable of comprehending the tremendous advantage that capital derives from the system, will bear its burdens without complaint."*
>
> - The Rothschild brothers of London writing to associates in New York, 1863.

The truth of the matter (and why you need to understand our modern banking system and how money is created) is that:

You need to begin to think and operate like a bank, or you're going to be a customer of the bank and be enslaved by the system.

The Biggest Hidden Tax Known to Man

We've lost 95% of the value of our dollar over the past 100 years (See Figure 2). Why is this? Prior to the creation of the Federal Reserve, you had very stable prices. The Federal Reserve System functions more like a banking cartel as evidenced by the fact that the Federal Reserve *has a complete* monopoly on the creation and control of the nation's money supply. The truth is that the Fed now exists solely to provide the inflation necessary to allow the government to spend more than it collects in taxes.

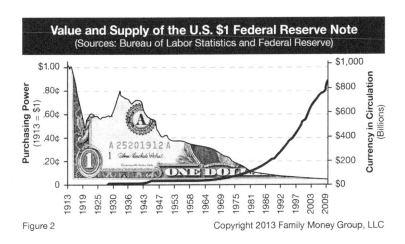

Figure 2   Copyright 2013 Family Money Group, LLC

Man has been plagued throughout history with the false theory that an increased money supply is better than less money in circulation. From the very beginning, the desire for a large money supply has ultimately been destructive to every civilization that has gone down the path of monetizing its debt (printing money with nothing of value behind it).

Inflation is the biggest hidden tax known to man. What the general public would never tolerate through direct taxation, they unknowingly submit to through inflation.

When the Fed, through its open market operations, injects money into the economy, they are diluting the economic "soup" and thus "watering it down." It's simple supply and demand economics. If the supply of something is greater in an economy, the value will go down. If the supply is less, the value goes up.

The creation of money is great for Wall Street, bankers, politicians, Ivy League academia, the World Bank and all those who run in these very close circles. Make no mistake about it, this is great for the privileged few who are near the top of the money spout. They have access to the money first. But you and I, who are down here on Main Street (near the bottom of the money spout), feel the very real effects of inflation by the time we get our hands on it.

We see and feel it (inflation) when we pay $4 for a gallon of milk. Or $6 a gallon if you are like my wife who insists on organic milk. By the way, we buy the generic value brand! Most of us don't realize *why* we're paying that much – we just figure that prices must have gone up.

Inflation has the *appearance* of rising prices, but in reality, the purchasing power of our money is going down.
They call it "inflation." The truth is something very different altogether.

The contraction/expansion of the money supply is the root cause of much of our economic woes. Now you know the true cause of the famous economic boom-bust cycles that we all hear about. So what I'm getting at here is the big idea of this book:

When you can create your own personal monetary system where 30% of your income is no longer contributing to the expansion of our money supply (see page 42, second paragraph), you become part of the solution, not the problem. This is when you begin to establish your own methods to finance your future and Retire Without Risk in a way that guarantees you'll have income for life.

Reread that last paragraph. It's imperative that you understand this because your future is at stake. The Government and Wall Street don't want you to know these things. They'd prefer you listen to their dogma and keep sending your money to them in the hopes of getting it back some day. Always remember:

Your Best Defense is an Informed Mind.

It is important for you to understand how money is created and what is really going on. Understanding our monetary system, banking, and economics will serve you well in these less than certain economic times.

Henry Ford once stated,

"It is well that the people of the nation do not understand our banking and monetary system, for if they did, I believe there would be a revolution before tomorrow morning."

Questions regarding the origin of money or the mechanism of its creation are seldom matters that the general public understands.

Why is this?

Answer: *"They" don't want you to know.*

In order for you to make wise decisions regarding your finances so you can Retire Without Risk, you'll want to join the ranks of the well informed.

If what you thought to be true about your money
turned out not to be,
when would you want to know?

The Bucket Brigade

Basically there are two ways to fill up a bucket with holes:

1. You can *increase* the flow, or
2. You can *plug* the holes and the bucket will fill even if it's just a trickle.

I use the term "bucket brigade" because it reminds me of the time when, to put out a fire, the community would form a line and pass buckets from the water supply to the fire and back. This worked well, unless the buckets had holes in them.

Any holes that you have in your wealth accumulation plan should be addressed *before* proceeding to pour more money into your financial "bucket." These "holes" are the many ways that you transfer your money to others (i.e. taxes, interest paid to others, debt, and the associated lost opportunity costs).

Once you've addressed these issues, and have plugged the holes, it will very quickly begin to have a substantial impact on your ability to accumulate wealth.

It is important to identify and avoid the *unnecessary* wealth transfers—the money you are currently giving away unknowingly and unnecessarily. *Identifying and plugging the holes in your bucket will have a far greater impact on your financial future than ever focusing on trying to get a higher rate of return and taking unnecessary risks.*

Consider the following example:

Annual Income	$102,000
Annual Savings	$10,200
Rate of Return on Savings	5%
Interest on Savings	$510
Annual Expenses	$91,800

As you can see, if someone makes $102,000 per year and they save 10% of their income at 5%, that $10,200 invested for one year would earn a whopping $510.00.

What does the typical conversation revolve around when you sit down with an advisor? "Well Mr. Investor, I think that I can get you a 7% rate of return."

Annual Income	$102,000
Annual Savings	$10,200
Rate of Return on Savings	7%
Interest on Savings	$714
Annual Expenses	$91,800

As you can see, going from 5% to 7% earned an extra $204 that year.

Instead, what if the focus was on reducing wealth transfers (plugging the holes)? If you could eliminate just 3% of money that you were losing unnecessarily, that would be the equivalent of a 27% rate of return on what you are already saving! Chasing higher rates of return is risky. *Reducing areas of risk and loss isn't.*

Reducing Expenses by just 3%	Saves in Dollars	Return equivalent on $10,200 invested	Which can be proven by the fact that:	Proof
3%	$2,754	27%	27% of $10,200 is:	$2,754

The bottom line is that your wealth is going to grow, regardless of whom you decide to work with. But, the reality is if you don't associate with somebody who understands these issues (and knows how to solve them) these problems will grow right along with your money and your bucket will never be as full as it could be, and you'll expose yourself to more risk than you need to.

The five biggest wealth transfers (which I address in detail later in the book) you need to be concerned with are:

1. Taxes

2. Your Mortgage

3. Your approach to college funding

4. The way you handle life's major purchases

5. Qualified Plans

You Finance Everything You Buy

What comes to mind when you read the above statement? You are probably thinking to yourself, no I don't!

Perhaps you recently paid cash for your kitchen remodel or that new bedroom furniture set you had been eyeing for some time. Did you make a choice to pay cash for your new car, or maybe it was for a new washer and dryer set?

When it comes to self-employed business owners, there's no doubt that they routinely pay cash for major capital purchases within their business.

Regardless of the business or personal item you decided to pay cash for, you thought it was a wise decision. The bottom line is that if you paid cash, you made a choice to use your money instead of someone else's money (borrowing to make your purchase). Paying cash for life's big-ticket items seemingly is a wise financial choice.

> The way you spend your money is equally as important as the act of actually saving your money.

Have you noticed that you always give up something when you make choices? For every financial choice you make, a sacrifice must be made to obtain something else that you consider more desirable. For example, you might forgo buying something today to invest those funds for future purchases. Or you might gain the use of an expensive item now by making credit payments from future earnings. You are constantly making choices among various financial decisions. In making those choices, you must consider the time value of money. This is basically the increase in the amount of money you would have as a result of the interest your money would earn if you didn't use it for this purchase.

Three Types of People

There are 3 Types of People in the world:

1. The Debtor

2. The Saver

3. The Wealth Creator

The Debtor: This person lives paycheck to paycheck. They don't have any savings, so they're at the mercy of the creditor. They pay the highest interest rates to someone else's bank.

They don't have savings; the only thing they have is their job, which they use as collateral. They pledge a portion of their future earnings to get a car. This person has no other option but to borrow to get what they want today.

Then there's **The Saver**: Make no mistake about it, this person is a borrower. If you save and pay cash for your purchases, you *are* a borrower; you just don't realize it.

Let me give you an example: if you pay $15,000 to remodel your kitchen and you take it out of your savings, you have just "borrowed" from yourself. Now I know plenty of people who, over a series of weeks, months or years will pay that $15,000 back to themselves. They depleted their cash reserves—their bucket—to remodel their kitchen, so now they are refilling their bucket. They're paying themselves back by saving money once again in a checking or savings account.

They've borrowed this $15,000 from themselves and they are studiously paying themselves back. Now, here's how our human nature works: I know plenty of people who will put back the money they took out ($15,000), but how many will pay back the *interest* they would have earned while the money was out of their account? Isn't that how much you would have had to repay had you taken a loan from a bank to remodel? Again, you need to begin to think and operate like a bank or you're always going to be a customer of the bank.

The other issue at work here is the lost compounded interest that this $15,000 would have created had it not been taken out. By spending it you are "killing the miracle" and financing someone else's future instead of your own.

The last type of person is the **Wealth Creator**: This person recognizes the power of leveraging other people's money (OPM). This allows them to keep their bucket full, make lifestyle purchases, and still have the liquidity, use and control of their own money.

They understand the miracle of compounding interest, and they don't kill the miracle. So *their* money continues to compound uninterrupted. The wealth creator borrows from any number of sources, including contractually guaranteed loans as one option, so that their money continues to grow, uninterrupted, over time.

Since wealth creators operate as their own bank using their own Personal Monetary System they aren't subject to having to convince the lender to give them a loan, and there are no hoops to jump through. The loans are guaranteed, no questions asked. The Wealth Creator leverages their personal monetary system to remodel their kitchen so that *their* money will continue to earn interest uninterrupted. When the wealth creator pays back the money they borrowed, not only do they have the $15,000 still in their possession (the principal amount that would have gone to the bank from their bucket—although they'd never do this because then that money would be gone forever and they'd lose all ability to use it again and again), but they also benefit by gaining from the additional interest and dividends that would have gone to someone else's bank. So after they repay this loan from their Personal Monetary System, they end up with a beautifully remodeled kitchen and still have the $15,000 of principal they started with, plus all of the interest that would have gone to someone else's bank. In addition, they potentially receive any dividends that would have gone to the bank's shareholders. That same money can now be used over and over again to make other lifestyle purchases in this same manner.

When the Wealth Creator pays back their loan, they get back not only all of the principal that *would have gone* to the bank, but also all the interest that would have also gone to the bank.

Remember that their money continued to earn interest because they have learned to use OPM to fund major expenditures. This is how banks earn money (charging you interest for the money they loan to you), and once you learn the system I'm about to explain and you begin to think and operate like a bank, you'll be able to do exactly the same thing.

Wealth Creators understand how to spend the same dollar over and over and over. Maybe this is why I say, "The Wealth Creator has learned to make their $1 earn $10, instead of what Wall Street has taught many people, which is how to make their $10 earn $1."

For the typical debtor and the majority of Americans, 30% of their income is going out the door to someone else's bank. Whether it is in the form of mortgage interest, credit card payments, student loans, car payments, or any other type of loan, the real problem is the volume of interest you are paying to the banking system. The reality is that many people are chasing higher rate of returns in their investments, while they are losing 30% of their income to some bank. Instead, you should learn to control the flow of your money and stop transferring it away to a system built to keep you coming back for more.

The need for finance is great throughout our entire life. If you can solve the finance equation, you'll be able to finance your *own* future and create your own Personal Monetary System. Solving the finance equation has far greater implications on your wealth creating potential than chasing higher rates of return and taking unnecessary risks.

And the secret from going from a saver to a Wealth Creator is learning how to create your own Personal Monetary System.

Strategies used by the Wealthiest 1%

Some of these ideas may be so foreign to you or may be such new concepts that you're thinking, "Why have I never heard about these?" It's because these are _uncommon_ strategies.

I'm going to illustrate this with something I like to call the income game; don't worry, there's no test.

Which of the following income categories would you say you would need to be in to be considered a top wage earner?

(Place an "x" on the appropriate line)

Top 1% _____   Top 5% _____   Top 10% _____

Top 20% _____   Top 25% _____

Now, complete the chart on the next page.

In the blanks below, write in what income you think someone needs to earn annually in order to fall into the top 1%, 5%, 10%, 25% and 50% of all wage earners in the United States:

1%	$
5%	$
10%	$
25%	$
50%	$

Once you have input your best guess above, turn to page 46 to see the real numbers.

Is Your household income common, or uncommon?

Turn the page to find out.

Just the facts…. These are the real stats…..

1%	$369,691
5%	$161,579
10%	$116,623
25%	$69,126
50%	$34,338

Data derived from Internal Revenue Service Tax Statistics

How close was your guess? Many people assume someone needs to earn hundreds of millions to be in the top 1%-10% of wage earners in the U.S.

To this point in your life you may have believed that your income was very common, but as you now see, based on where your income falls in these categories, if you're in the top 25%, your income is *uncommon*. You may have *thought* it was common because you go to church with people who make similar incomes, you live in a neighborhood with people who make similar incomes, and you're around people at work who make similar incomes. People tend to run with people who are in the same economic circles. The reality is that if you are in the top 10%, you earn more than 9 out of 10 people in the U.S. If your annual household income is at least $69,126 you earn more than 75% of the general population. If you are in the top 25% or higher, is your income common or uncommon?

Answer: *Un*common.

If your income is *uncommon*, should you be listening to financial advice that relies on common strategies available to everyone and promoted by most advisors and Wall Street?

OR, should you be using the more *uncommon* strategies the Wealth Creators have been using for decades?

What I'm sharing with you are the *uncommon* strategies that the wealthy have been using for decades to build tax-free wealth, tax-free retirement and guaranteed income for life.

Look back on your life and ask, "What strategies have I been employing in my financial life?" Are you the Debtor, the Saver, or the Wealth Creator? Wealth Creators know two things for certain:

1. Exactly how much money they're going to have in retirement (and it's guaranteed),

2. They will never outlive their money.

Wealth Creators know exactly how much they'll receive each and every month (long before they get to retirement age) and they know they are going to receive it for the rest of their life – guaranteed!

They've created their own Guaranteed Retirement System. And through the rest of this book, I'll show you how to create *your* own Guaranteed Retirement System by using these *uncommon* strategies known to Wealth Creators.

I'm from the Government and I'm here to help with your 401(k)

© Wiley Ink, inc./Distributed by Universal Uclick via CartoonStock.com

Do you remember Ronald Reagan's famous quote about the nine most terrifying words:

"I'm from the government and I'm here to help."

You can bet that anytime politicians or bureaucrats advocate something under the auspices of protecting you, most likely you will be harmed, not helped.

You must know that the vast majority of politicians in Washington see your investment account or your 401(k) not as the expressions of well-planned disciplined decisions on your part, but as untapped reservoirs of wealth they can drain to fix the problems they have caused.

For most Americans, the "default" or primary vehicle they use to save for their retirement is through their government qualified plans, 401(k), 403(b), SEP, etc. The problem with this is that the government created all those plans and the government can change the rules at any time and there is nothing you can do about it. The term "qualified" indicates that the plan is governed by the Employee Retirement Income Security Act (ERISA).

As Social Security continues to have problems and the government sees a need to generate more revenue, where do you think they will go? Some of that money in your qualified plan is not yours – it rightfully belongs to the government because they were kind enough to make your contributions "tax deferred." That means that you didn't have to pay taxes on that money when you put it in, but you will when you take it out in the future.

Who's to say that the government won't determine that they need "their portion" of your 401(k) to help fund Social Security or some other program? What if they decide to tax the gains in your Roth IRA? All of the contributions in a Roth IRA are made with after-tax dollars with the promise that any growth in your money would not be subject to the federal income tax. Think that can't happen? Your Social Security "contributions" are made with after-tax dollars, and it was promised that those benefits would be tax free, but Washington started chipping away at that vow back in the

1980s. Today, millions of Social Security recipients find a portion of their benefits subject to the IRS. It's "their money" after all.

Can you see why I'm not a big believer in having the majority of your retirement savings in a government created vehicle? Keep reading and I'll tell you how to avoid this very dangerous (and soon to be real) trap.

Washington's lust for Americans' retirement investments is very real.

In fact, the headlines are filled with stories about politicians' desires to further control your money. Recently, the new Consumer Financial "Protection" Bureau (which is a new federal agency created as a result of the Dodd-Frank Act) has made it known that they are eyeing your retirement accounts. Don't make the mistake and believe they have your best interest in mind. They want your money.

It is no secret that our federal debt is growing at a breakneck speed. Our federal government is borrowing over $40,000 per second *more* than they bring in through tax revenues. $40,000 per second! By the time you read the next few pages, our country will have amassed close to one hundred million dollars of new debt. By the time you finish this book, it's well over a billion dollars!

A few months back I interviewed William Beach from The Heritage Foundation's Center for Data Analysis. Specifically, William and I discussed the recently released Index of Dependence on Government. Yes, there is such a report! You can listen to my interview with William Beach by going to: DLShowOnline.com. Here are a few facts that I found very disturbing:

The percentage of people who do not pay federal income taxes and who are not claimed as dependents by someone who does pay them, jumped from 14.8% in 1984 to 49.5% in 2009. This means that in 1984, 34.8 million tax filers paid no taxes; in 2009, 151.7 million people paid no federal taxes! (Yes, you read that right!) This poses the question, how long can our form of representative government survive in light of these facts? I'm a numbers person. To me it is simple mathematics. Something has to give.

I have come to the conclusion that one thing is certain: Our taxes will go up in the future.

These are serious issues that must be addressed in relation to where one decides to accumulate money.
In the very near future, about two-thirds of the now-working population will be 60 years old or older. Undoubtedly, this leaves one-third of the now-working population to pay for all the government entitlement programs for a majority of retired citizens. To add fuel to the fire, the costs of these social programs such as Social Security and Medicare, are rapidly increasing. It is unlikely that politicians will make the tough choices that are necessary to keep these programs solvent. This leaves little doubt that increased taxation will be the course of action they will take to keep these programs afloat. As I write this, it appears that The Affordable Care Act (AKA: Obama Care) is a logistical and fiscal train wreck. In typical form and fashion of a government program, it will cost many times the projected cost to implement and it will only make things worse.

It is estimated that by 2040, the elderly population will represent 20.7% of the total population. The largest segment of the population that grew the fastest was people between the ages of 90 and 94. Remember, my own grandmother is turning 99 this year and she still lives at home by herself! This age group has increased 44.6% since 1990. To give you some perspective, in 1900 the average life expectancy was 47.3 years.

Along with shifting age demographics, the government itself plays a role in eroding our future wealth. Over the last 40+ years, the only thing the government has been successful at is overspending the amount they've taken in. Recently they raised the amount of money you can put into the government qualified retirement plans. Why? Was this change implemented because they were concerned about *your* financial future...or *theirs*? A 401(k) or IRA simply defers taxation to a later date. *At first, it may appear that you save on taxes, but most likely you won't.*

If all things are equal, meaning your rate of return and the rate at which you are taxed are the same today and when you retire, THERE IS NO DIFFERENCE between pre-tax and after-tax contributions. You will end up with the EXACT same amount of money. This is a mathematical certainty.

If you postpone paying your taxes to a later date, essentially you are subject to a future unknown tax calculation that you have no control over. Only the government decides how much they are going to take.

Take a look at USDebtClock.org and decide for yourself if you think taxes are going up, staying the same or going down in the future. If you believe that taxes are going up in the future, then deferring your taxes to a later date is a bad idea.

In light of this country's shifting demographics, as well as the massive increases in government debt, you need to know one thing is certain: Higher taxes will be waiting for you in the future. Many people take the advice of the government and their advisors. They are lead to believe that postponing their taxes to a future date at an unknown calculation makes a lot of sense.

Doing this can be likened to going to meet with your banker and asking to borrow some money. Your banker happily tells you that he has plenty of money. He tells you he has drawn up your loan paperwork. There is just one little detail. The bank he works for isn't sure what their future internal expenses will be, therefore the bank will notify you in the future just how much interest they need to charge you. Would you take that loan? Of course not! Yet, isn't this what you do when you participate in a qualified plan? Now, there is one exception. If you are receiving a match from your employer, it may be to your advantage to contribute. I emphasize the word "*may*".

Many people are unaware that there are options available that allow them to accumulate their savings tax-free as well as spend their savings tax-free.

A dollar in taxes paid unnecessarily not only costs you what you lost, but also what that dollar could have earned--had you not transferred it away.

Here's another thing I have never understood. Why does the Government penalize you if you need access to your money before you are 59 ½?? Sometimes you may need your money, but when it's locked up in a government qualified plan, it's almost impossible to access it.

Consider this: With common qualified retirement plans you effectively lock up your money for the next 40 years (assuming you start saving at age 20 – see Figure 3). If you do want access to your money, you are going to pay a 10% penalty (in addition to your regular tax bill) to get to your money. Once you finally reach 59 ½ you enter into a magical eleven-year period where you have access to your money and are not subject to any penalties. During these eleven years, you can take out as much or as little as you wish without the government penalizing you. However, when you turn 70 ½, you are forced to take out what is called a required minimum distribution (RMD). The government wants their fair share. If you don't take out your RMD, you will be penalized up to a 50% increase in taxes on the money you should have taken out, but didn't. Now, if you live another 20 years, you are in a penalty phase 80-85% of the time. This poses the question:

Who was this plan designed for? You and your family?

No! It was designed for Uncle Sam.

Age: 20		Age: 59.5	Age: 70.5
	40 YEARS	11 YEARS	20 YEARS
401K/IRA TAX QUALIFIED	**10% PENALTY** FOR WITHDRAW PLUS INCOME TAX	**NO PENALTY** PAY INCOME TAX	**50% PENALTY TO HOLD** PAY INCOME TAX

When you save in a Qualified Plan/IRA you are subject to penalties for up to 85% of the life of the plan!

Figure 3

It is important that you have complete liquidity, use, and control of your money while at the same time you continue to earn uninterrupted compounding interest. This is how Wealth Creators operate.

The government doesn't want you to worry about the pain of paying unnecessary taxes. You need to gain more knowledge so you are capable of making better financial decisions. The more you know, the less pain you will suffer financially. The solutions to a prosperous financial future are not found by speculating in the market, although that's what most people believe.

Why?

Because it's what they've been taught from childhood. It is difficult to get the right solution when you start out with the wrong premise. The government sees you as a taxpayer... it's how they fund their insatiable appetite for spending.

So whose future are you financing?

Yours...or the governments?

3 Retirement Goals

Most people I talk with have three overarching goals for their retirement years:

1. Income for Life that is Guaranteed,

2. Long Term Care Provision (whether you are well enough to continue living in your home, or if you have to reside in a long-term care facility, it's expensive to have someone care for you. This is a real concern with most people I talk to.)

3. To leave a tax-free Inheritance to their children or favorite charity.

The most common way people save for retirement is through a common strategy using a 401(k) or other qualified plan. This is because Wall Street and the government have successfully convinced Americans that this is the primary vehicle to save for retirement. Now, based on what you've learned up to this point, WHY do you think they want you to do this? (Answer: because they control the banking system and have access to your money when they need it).

The bottom line is that your "Qualified plan" could become *dis*qualified in the very near future. What would that do to your retirement plan?

The Federal Government gets to determine how much they want to take and when they want to take it. When they find themselves in "need" of more money, where do you think they will go next?

There's nothing worse than saving for your retirement only to have someone else change the rules near the end of the game.

In light of these harsh realities, here's a question to ask yourself:

Do you believe taxes are:

a. Going to go down,
b. Going to stay about the same, or
c. Going to go up?

If they're going to go up, it's a losing strategy to defer your taxes to a date when they are higher; why would you want to do that? If they're going to go down in the future, it's a winning strategy. You decide. Which direction do you think that taxes are heading in the future?

The government knows how to market. They should call qualified plans what they really are which are tax postponement plans.

> Death and taxes are a certainty. While we have little to no control over the former, we can and should be proactive about the latter.

Is the same Federal government that has social security headed for bankruptcy looking to mess with your 401(k) or IRA?

Absolutely! Don't be a slave to the government's monetary system. It's time to create your own Personal Monetary System.

Being a Crash Test Dummy

The problem with being a crash test dummy is that you're the guinea pig for someone else's hypothesis and most of the time, the results aren't pretty.

The fact is Wall Street does not want an informed public capable of the critical thinking necessary to make important financial decisions with the regards to their savings.

As you've just learned through the previous pages, Wall Street and the Government have created a system so complex and secretive that most of us on Main Street feel like dummies.

They've sold us a dream that someday, if we continue to invest and "weather the market storms" then we'll accumulate enough money to enjoy retirement. The problem with their hypothesis is that *they* are not the ones in the driver's seat getting ready to smash into the windshield at 120 mph. You and I are!

58

Wall Street and the Government are sitting in their "ivory tower" pushing the buttons that control this "game of chance." They come out the winners and we end up losing our life savings. I believe it's time to change the situation.

What I Learned from Saturday Morning TV

Many of us grew up on Saturday morning TV, watching the classic Schoolhouse Rock®. This is where we learned how to invest in the Stock Market. Perhaps you remember the song:

> "Buy low, Sell high, take a piece of the pie,
> that's the Wall Street way."

Well, that's where we learned how to get sucked into the system; the Wall Street Casino as I call it. This casino is where millions of Americans are gambling their future hoping for a larger return later in life.

The true lyrics of that song should be:

> "Buy low, sell high, kiss your money goodbye,
> that's the Wall Street way."

So, investing in the stock market is not the way Wealth Creators accumulate their wealth. They do it by creating their own Personal Monetary System. This system enables them to build wealth long-term *and* benefit today by having

CASH:

C – Compound Interest that Creates Wealth

A – Access to their Money Tax Free

S – Safe, Secure Investment with Guaranteed Returns

H – Heirs Receive an Inheritance Tax Free

When you have access to **CASH,** you can take advantage of investment opportunites today. Having access to **CASH** gives you use and control of your money today (tax free), while at the same time, you are earning uninterrupted compounding interest on your money. In the event of your untimely demise, your anticipated retirement account balance is fully funded on a tax-free basis. In other words, your unexpected death will not change all of the other hopes and dreams you and your family had together.

Driving on an Empty Tank

For the average person, the common strategy is to invest in the stock market, but a market "correction" can set you back, making it more difficult to stay ahead of your plan. These setbacks drain your savings "tank" and "kill the miracle" of compound interest.

Even one correction can hurt you. Multiple fluctuations will drastically slow you down, and could even bring you to a complete halt, much like trying to drive your car on an empty tank. The chart below is very telling. It reveals how much gain you would need to realize just to get back to square one – aka: break event point!

Gain Required to Recoup Your Principal	
% Lost	% Gain Needed to get back what you lost
20%	25%
30%	42.85%
40%	66.7%
50%	100%

The problem with these Wall Street retirement plans (or qualified plans as they are called), where most people are saving for retirement, is that the markets go up and down regularly. You have no control of the outcome.

However, when you create your own Personal Monetary System and establish your Guaranteed Retirement System, it only goes one way...UP.

And you will always know the exact answer to those three greatest retirement issues facing most of us:
Guaranteed Income for Life
Long-Term Care Protection, and
Leaving a tax-free Inheritance to Your Children.

When you are saving for your retirement, you want to drive with a full tank. Don't allow anyone (i.e. Wall Street or the Government) to siphon your "fuel" through risky investments or market "corrections" that you cannot control.

It is much wiser for you to control your future by creating your own Personal Monetary System, which will include your Guaranteed Retirement System so that you will be able to Finance Your Future and Retire Without Risk.

The Wall Street Casino

I'm going to show you how to beat Wall Street at their own game.

These are Main Street strategies to beat Wall Street.

These are common sense strategies that produce *uncommon* returns, just like the Wealth Creators. These are the insider's secrets of the wealthy in America that you can apply now.

Let's say we were going to send you to the Masters Golf Tournament and we made you this offer:

You can choose one of these two things:

1. **The clubs** of any player that has ever played a round of golf, or
2. **The ability** of any player that has ever played a round of golf.

Which would you choose?

Of course you'd choose their ability!

It's not the clubs that make the player. It's the player's ability that makes the club.

What is it that financial institutions have to offer? They have products to sell, which we will call the clubs. Do you need clubs to play the game? Of course you do, but the greatest impact on your game comes more from your ability to play the game than it does from having the right club. So becoming a Wealth Creator is less about the clubs (the products that are offered) and more about the process you go through to use the clubs.

In short: It's more about the process than any product.

To become a Wealth Creator, you need to think and operate like a bank, otherwise you'll be a customer of the bank. Continue to read and you'll learn *how* you can begin to think and operate like a bank by creating your own Personal Monetary System.

Safe Deposit Boxes

Q: Where do people keep their safe deposit box?

A: At the bank. (Someone else's bank.)

Q: And what do they keep in that safe deposit box?

A : Valuables, documents and cash.

Q: Where do _banks_ hold their safest investments?
(In other words, _Where_ is the bank's safe deposit box?)

A: Banks hold their valuables (cash) in BOLIs.
(BOLI = Bank Owned Life Insurance)

Most people have no idea that many banks own massive amounts of permanent cash value life insurance. They do so because it's a very safe investment vehicle.

Banks don't speculate with their money. They want to convince you to put your money in a straitjacket for the next 30 years, or until you reach "retirement age" (as determined by the government at that time). Remember, if you need access to your money before age 59 ½, they will charge you a 10% penalty on top of your already sizable tax bill. This virtually assures them that you will keep your money in the market while they earn substantial fees year in and year out. Those fees are guaranteed to be there...your money is not!

When I refer to banks and their insatiable appetite to speculate with your money, I am primarily talking about the banks that are too big to fail. Let me define "too big to fail." I mean banks whose owners and managers believe themselves to be exempt from the *processes* of bankruptcy. These too-big-to-fail financial institutions capture the financial upside of their actions, but largely avoid bankruptcy and insolvency—for foolish actions gone wrong. In other words, they have successfully privatized their profits and socialized trillions in losses (they get to keep the money, we get to pay for it). This, of course, contradicts one of the basic tenets of free market capitalism (certainly as it is should be practiced in the United States). These big banks enjoy subsidies and explicit guarantees that their competitors do not. Therefore, they are likely to take more risks in pursuit of profits, protected by the presumption that bankruptcy is a highly unlikely outcome.

> *"Capitalism without failure is like religion without sin—it just doesn't work."*
>
> - Allan Maultzer, Economist

As of late 2012, there were roughly 5,600 commercial banking organizations in the U.S. The majority of these—approximately 5,500—were community banks with assets of less than $10 billion. These small, community-focused banks accounted for 98.6% of all banks, but just 12% of the banking industry's total assets. At the other end of the scale are the megabanks—with assets of between $250 billion and $2.3 trillion. This group is made up of a mere 12 banks. These twelve behemoths account for roughly 0.2% of all banks, but they hold nearly 70% of all the industry's assets! There is an inextricable link between these megabanks, Wall Street and the desire for your money.

It is also important to note that with the repeal of the Glass-Steagall Act, many of these Investment Banking Firms are now owned by the Giant "Too-Big-To-Fail" Banks that continue to receive taxpayer subsidies (i.e., Bank of America now owns Merrill Lynch).

Banks don't speculate with *their* money, but they do want to speculate with your money. They take your money and then they "take it off the table" (much like the casinos in Vegas). They invest a large amount of your money (it *was* your money, now it's theirs) in something that is called a BOLI, or bank- owned life insurance.

In a recent 24-month period, banks increased their holdings in bank-owned life insurance (BOLI), by over 40 BILLION dollars. In fact, Citibank® and its subsidiary bought over $1 Billion in cash value life insurance (BOLI) within a 9-month period. When things are going bad, the banking industry doesn't invest over $40 Billion in something that is bad for them or is a risky investment.

- Why would banks purchase BOLIs (cash value life insurance policies)?

- Because it provides them immense economic and financial benefits, stability and safety that is guaranteed!

At the same time that Citibank® snapped up over $1 Billion of high cash value life insurance in a nine month period, Primerica (at the time a wholly owned subsidiary of Citibank®) had a website promoting that you should purchase life insurance. If you went to the website of Primerica at that time, do you know what they would have told you to do??

"Buy term and invest the rest."

Note the irony... Citibank® bought over $1 Billion of *cash value* life insurance (not term life insurance), but they are advising you to "buy term and invest the rest." Don't you find that to be a bit strange?? Why would they do this?

Again, going back to what we we've been talking about; the banks want to speculate with *your* money.

When you "buy term and invest the rest," *they* earn money when you dump your money in risky financial products (clubs). YOU are losing control and use of your money while they earn fees, even if your account goes down! They love this! You shouldn't!

To this day, the banks "safe deposit box" as it were – where *they* store *their* money for a guaranteed safe, long-term return—is in one of the safest investments known to man. Up to 25% of many banks' Tier 1 Capital Assets (their safest type of asset) reside in BOLIs or high cash value life insurance.

If banks use cash value life insurance as one of their safest investments, shouldn't you?

Remember: to become a Wealth Creator, you need to think and operate like a bank.

If you would like to validate much of this information and data, I encourage you to read the book *The Pirates of Manhattan* by Barry Dyke. Barry has done extensive research on the topics of where banks invest their money. You can also listen to me interview Barry Dyke here: DLShowOnline.com/books.

Life insurance is one of the most misunderstood financial vehicles even though it has been in existence for over 150 years. What many people don't realize is that owning a properly structured cash value policy through a mutually held dividend- paying Life Insurance Company offers a multitude of living benefits. It's not just about the death benefits!

The reality is that 95% of insurance agents don't understand how to properly structure a policy to assist you in creating your own Personal Monetary System. Those agents don't help their clients implement these strategies for one of two reasons:

1. *Commissions.* A properly structured cash value life insurance policy that emphasizes cash accumulation and living benefits directly *reduces* commissions paid to a life insurance agent by 60% or more. It's a sad, but true, reality. In the sales world, incentive drives behavior. This is one reason many consumers are not aware such a powerful financial tool exists.

2. *Wall Street, and the major financiers of the financial media want you to be convinced that you would be a fool if you ever send a dollar to a life insurance company to allow them to invest it for you.* (Every dollar that goes to an insurance company does not go to Wall Street). Unfortunately many advisors have been conditioned to tell you to "buy term and invest the rest." It also may very well be that they simply do not understand how to properly structure a high cash value policy to help you maximize the living benefits while retaining the death benefit.

There is a behind-the-scenes battle that has been taking place for some time. Wall Street lost credibility with the American saver after The Great Depression. The average person had little desire to gamble their life savings by speculating it on Wall Street. Wall Street realized things had to change if they were to ever get their hands on people's money.

In the late 1970s, Wall Street heavily lobbied congress to change the laws. In 1974, Wall Street was successful in their efforts with the passage of the Employment Retirement Income Securities Act (ERISA). Prior the passage of the ERISA, it was commonplace for someone to work for a company their entire working life. In exchange, the worker would receive a guaranteed pension payment for the rest of their lives. To this day, and for the last 30 years, my living grandmother receives a small pension check from my grandfather's employer.

Essentially ERISA changed everything. As a result, from that day forward, most Americans became their own pension fund manager. It became the do-it-yourself retirement system. The default employment retirement savings plan made the American Saver responsible for their own retirement, but with no guarantees.

Wall Street's success culminated in 1980 with the introduction of the 401(k), which was the primary tool to capture millions in profits and yet provide no guarantees of any nature as to the outcome for the retirement saver. Once they gained access to all this money through automatic payroll deductions, Wall Street knew they had hit a gold mine.

If you would like to learn more about the history of retirement in America, be sure to read the book *The Great Wall Street Retirement Scam* by Rick Bueter*. You can also listen to me interview Rick at: DLShowOnline.com/Books.

You see, the insurance-based retirement system has been around for hundreds of years and has withstood the test of time. At the turn of the century, nearly 50% of American's discretionary savings were held by life insurance companies. Savers liked the fact that they offered something that banks and Wall Street could not: the safety and security that their money was never at risk.

Life insurance companies are masters at managing money and economic risk. They're all about giving maximum guarantees with maximum returns.

During the great depression, when 10,000 banks failed, the facts revealed that 99.9% of money deposited with life insurance companies was found to be safe. In fact, during this time period, it was life insurance companies that provided the capital to help banks stabilize, not the federal government

Insurance companies don't gamble with their money or yours. In fact, with a mutually held life insurance company, you can actually receive dividends, which are considered a return of premium. You essentially become an owner in the company and can benefit from the profits they earn.

*See recommended reading list on page 132

Mailbox Money

Every day insurance companies are mailing millions of dollars to mailboxes across the country... and they will continue to do this every month—guaranteed. This money comes from cash value life insurance policies and very specialized insurance contracts called annuities.

Although annuities have only existed in their present form for a few decades, the idea of paying out a stream of income to an individual or family dates back to the Roman Empire. The Latin word "annua" meant annual stipends. During the reign of the emperors the word signified a contract that made annual payments. Individuals would make a single large payment into the annua and then receive an annual payment each year until death, or for a specified period of time.

In the 1930s annuities became very popular as concerns about the overall health of the financial markets prompted many individuals to purchase products from insurance companies. In the midst of the Great Depression, insurance companies were seen as stable institutions that could make the guaranteed payouts they'd promised. In fact, the legendary baseball player Babe Ruth invested his life savings in annuities during the depression and never lost a single penny.

It is important to note that today's annuities provide consumers with what they want: more options. The annuities of today are very different from annuities of the past. These highly specialized insurance contracts give the consumer maximum control and flexibility, including a guaranteed paycheck for life that can never be outlived.

Here's how this works:

1. When you or your spouse dies, the surviving spouse has many choices including:

   a. Being paid a penalty-free lump sum of the remaining funds that have not been spent.

   b. Elect to continue to receive the guaranteed income stream for the remainder of the surviving spouse's life. Remember, the surviving spouse cannot outlive this money. They will receive this money each and every month, guaranteed. Even if their account has been depleted to zero!

After the death of both spouses, if there is any money left over, in most states it bypasses probate and passes to their beneficiary with absolutely no penalties! In other words, the entire proceeds they leave their heirs would go to them without the insurance company charging any fees before their beneficiary receives the proceeds.

Every day, the amount of guaranteed income that insurance companies mail to people rivals what the Federal Government mails out in benefit checks. Millions of dollars are mailed daily to people who have been wise enough to avoid putting the bulk of their assets at risk.

These people are enjoying what we all long for:

Guaranteed Income for Life and

Retirement Without Risk.

The Life Insurance industry has not strained the American taxpayer with unending, taxpayer subsidies, unlike the "too big to fail" banks.

Only the insurance-based system of retirement can provide you with your own private pension plan or what I like to call Mailbox Money. The returns paid on these plans are guaranteed to go in only one direction; UP!

Your money Is never at risk.

(See Figure 3 on the next page)

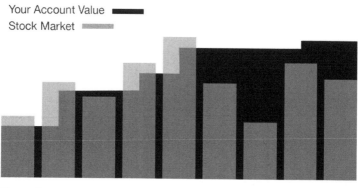

Your Account Value ▬
Stock Market ▬

Figure 3   Copyright 2013 Family Money Group, LLC

It is Wall Street that has fooled so many into believing that they must speculate and take risks with their life's savings to build a substantial retirement income stream.

Wall Street...

- Cannot and Will Not Guarantee that you won't outlive your money.

- They Cannot and Will Not Guarantee how much money you will receive *for the rest of your life.*

The Insurance Industry can, does and has provided these guarantees for generations.

> Question: Why didn't you know about this before?

> Answer: Wall Street didn't and still doesn't want you to know.

A recent study was published entitled "The 4 Percent Rule is Not Safe in a Low-Yield World." The study was conducted by Professor Michael Finke, Ph.D., CFP® who is a coordinator in the Department of Personal Financial Planning at Texas Tech University. Mr. Finke argues that advisers make a grave mistake in basing their client's retirement plans on historical returns that may be an anomaly.

Some highlights from the study that I found very interesting:

Investment companies often include in their disclosures that "past returns do not guarantee future results," but the study's co-author, Michael Finke, says that's not just rhetoric. "We're trying to acknowledge what present reality looks like and apply that reality to the retirement income plan." Finke says there is no reason to believe that the market for assets in the 21st century is going to look like the market for assets in the 20th century (remember the shifting demographics).

"Most planners take some comfort in knowing that the 4% inflation-adjusted withdrawal rate wouldn't cause a retiree to run out of money in a 30-year retirement. Previous studies that supported the 4% rate used historical yield data that don't look anything like what new retirees are facing today."

The study concludes that the probability of a retiree running out of money is very real and many financial planners are setting their clients up to run out of money.

Before the year 2000, there was a general consensus in the financial planning industry that a 6-8% annual withdrawal rate would provide a relative degree of certainty that a retiree wouldn't outlive their money. After the 2008 financial crisis, many experts are saying 2-3% is a safe bet. This is especially true if you have the bulk of your savings in the Wall Street casino.

Only today's insurance contracts can provide you with a guaranteed paycheck that you can never outlive. Another thing I would like to point out here is that Insurance companies hold a minimum of a dollar-for-dollar reserve. That means that they have a dollar in reserve for every dollar that they loan out.

Whereas in banking, banks are only required to hold a fraction of your deposits on reserve. So when you deposit $10,000 at your local bank, they can legally loan out $9,000 of your deposit to someone else. Banks are inherently unstable as evidenced by the fact that between the years of 1981 to 1996 approximately 2,900 banks failed in the U.S. and hundreds of banks have failed since 2008.

Many people are unaware that if just a small percentage of their bank's clientele demanded to withdraw cash at the same time, the money simply wouldn't be there. So if everybody did a run on the bank, it would be a very short race. The money is not there. Remember what happened to George Bailey in the movie *It's a Wonderful Life*? That's a very real scenario that could happen again if we hit major economic turbulence.

When there is a major shake in economic confidence, in any way, only a very small percentage of this money is actually in the form of paper Federal Reserve notes. The vast majority is digital money that exists only in electronic form. It's nothing more than a number.

The FDIC (Federal Deposit Insurance Corporation) currently insures deposits up to $250,000 per account. You can't miss the FDIC sign when you are making your deposit at the bank.

However, most people do not know that the FDIC currently has only 0.45% of reserves in their deposit insurance fund! (as of December 31, 2012). What does this mean to you? It means that for every $100 you deposit at your local bank, the FDIC has just *forty-five cents* to back it up! Another way of putting it, they have less than one penny for every dollar you have on deposit. The FDIC's goal is to reach 1.35% reserve ratios by September 30, 2020. This is not very reassuring!

With the state of our current economy, and the likely direction that taxes are heading, how confident are you that the money you are saving for retirement will actually be enough for you to live on for the rest of your life? Consider what you've read and you'll more fully appreciate three of my most frequently used statements:

1. The government has an insatiable appetite for your money.

2. Neither Wall Street nor the government wants an informed public.

3. Your best defense is an informed mind.

My hope is that by reading this book you will gain in understanding (become informed) and learn what it takes to keep your money from being devoured. By taking action now, you can eliminate stress and Retire Without Risk.

Creating Your Personal Monetary System

Many people *hope* to go to Hawaii sometime in their life. Others are actually *planning* to go to Hawaii. The difference is financing.

Some people talk like this:

> *"I hope to go to Hawaii because I hope the money is going to be there. I'm saving for my 30th Anniversary and I want to take my wife to Hawaii. I'm hoping we can go, but, because of the stock market's volatility and the uncertainty of new regulations, I'm not sure if we'll be able to go....*
> *And I can't touch the money I have in my IRA until I am 59 ½ or I'll pay an enormous penalty. I sure hope things work out."*

On the other hand, some of my clients talk like this:

> "I'm planning our 30th Anniversary trip to Hawaii.
> My wife and I have always wanted to go and since I
> know I have access to all my money for this trip, I'm
> going to surprise her with a vacation of a lifetime.
> And the other great thing is that we'll take this trip
> completely tax-free! It doesn't get any better than
> that!"

By having your own Personal Monetary System, you can
plan to go to Hawaii because you'll know the money will be
there and you will have complete access to it with flexible
repayment terms and your use of it is completely tax-free.

Remember the 3 primary goals most people have for
retirement:

1. Guaranteed income for life,
2. Long-term care planning
3. Leaving a tax-free legacy to their children.

You can achieve these 3 goals, AND go to Hawaii (or
anywhere else you'd like to go) when you think and operate
like a bank by creating your own Personal Monetary System.
It's at this point when you begin to Finance Your Future and
set yourself up to Retire Without Risk.

This is how successful Wealth Creators function. Wealth
Creators don't rely on what "they" say. Wealth Creators
function differently.

They don't "chase returns" *hoping* for a better result.
Wealth Creators plan for their future by financing major

purchases through their own Personal Monetary System.

These are the *uncommon* strategies that the wealthy have been using to create tax-free wealth for generations. Have you ever wondered why the Kennedys, Rockefellers and Hunts have been wealthy from generation to generation? It's because they understand and apply these strategies. Now you can too.

To create your own Personal Monetary System, you need to go through a very simple process:

1. Establish and capitalize your system
2. Borrow from your system
3. Repay your loan(s) with interest to your system

When you create your own Personal Monetary System, you will be able to avoid the traditional "system" that's been created by the government and Wall Street. You'll have complete control and access to your money and be able to Finance Your Future and Retire Without Risk as you accomplish the 3 Major Retirement Goals:

1. Guaranteed income for life,
2. Long-term Care Planning,
3. Leaving your heirs a tax-free inheritance.

The beauty of creating your Personal Monetary System is that you'll never "kill the miracle" of compound interest. You'll finance life's major expenditures using OPM (Other People's Money) and you'll retain all of the interest that you would have normally paid to someone else, thus increasing your wealth—all on a tax-free basis.

Your Personal Monetary System maximizes the 3 Types of Money. This unique method used by Wealth Creators allows you to have more:

Accumulated money for your retirement (using the very safe and tax sheltered vehicle that banks use),

Lifestyle money to enjoy life now and in the future (by giving you complete access and control of your money), and

Transferred money that stays in your possession as you retain the principal and earn interest you would have given to others.

To become a Wealth Creator—to Finance Your Future and Retire Without Risk—you need to think and operate like a bank. Creating a Personal Monetary System is the *un*common strategy used by many of America's wealthiest and most influential families. It's how they accumulate money for retirement, enjoy their lives today, and transfer wealth to their heirs instead of the government and financial institutions.

There are many ways for you to recapture the interest you are paying to others and save for major expenses you know you'll incur by using your Personal Monetary System. The following pages outline just a few of the major areas where you can "plug the holes in your bucket" and begin to accumulate wealth using your own Personal Monetary System.

Small Business, The Backbone of the American Economy

If you are a self-employed business owner, this chapter is dedicated to you! You wake up every day unemployed, and you don't get paid until someone says, "Yes, I want your product or service!"

> There is one thing that all business owners have in common. They want their business to grow!

The entrepreneurial spirit and the hard work that every business owner invests into their business is to be honored. The many hours of sacrifice, blood, sweat and tears behind the scenes that every entrepreneur experiences is to be commended. All of this energy is expended *without any guarantee of success.*

The small business owner is the primary job creator in this great country of ours and any success they achieve is despite all of the obstacles in front of them. They overcome these adversities to improve their lives, but also the lives of those they employ and ultimately those they serve. This is what makes America work (free markets without oppressive laws and regulations) not the bureaucrats in Washington D.C. If you work for a small business owner, thank them. If you are a small business owner, you know what I am talking about first hand. You did build that!

If you are a business owner who is reading this and you are discouraged, take a moment to read these quotes. I hope they will give you renewed optimism and determination to succeed.

I think it was Thomas Edison who once said, "Many people miss opportunity because it goes around wearing overalls and looks a lot like hard work." Here are a few of my other favorite quotes about business success:

> *"Business is full of brilliant men who started out with a spurt and lacked the stamina to finish. Their places were taken by patient and unshowy plodders who never knew when to quit."*
>
> ~J.R. Todd

> *"A pessimist sees the difficulty in every opportunity; an optimist sees the opportunity in every difficulty."*
>
> ~ Winston Churchill

> *"Obstacles are those frightful things you see when you take your eyes off your goal."*
>
> ~Henry Ford

> *"Never, Never, Never Give Up."*
>
> ~Winston Churchill

Question: What is the common advice and strategy that most small business owners are receiving from financial advisors?

Answer: Put your money into a SEP, IRA or other qualified plans.

For the business owner, there is one major flaw with these common investment vehicles that are encouraged by many financial planners:

Lack of liquidity! As a business owner, you lose the ability to use and control your money. You can't touch your money until you are 59 ½. That's not good.

Advisors have all kinds of ideas about where you should be investing the money your business is generating, but when it comes down to it, I believe that the first place a business owner should focus investing their money is within their own business. This is because their business is something they have an intimate knowledge of and a relative degree of control over.

Business owners are typically focused so much on the profitability of their business that they overlook expenses lost along the way. Now I'm not talking about the money that your business is forced to spend which is simply a cost of doing business. Expenses also consist of money that you are losing unknowingly and unnecessarily.

Consider this example of a business:

Annual Operating Expense	$1,000,000
Annual Outside Investment	$25,000
O.I. Rate of Return	5.00%
Annual O.I. Growth	$1,250

This example on page 84 assumes that the annual expenses for this business is one million dollars. The business owner is currently investing $25,000 outside of his business to save for retirement, etc. If he experiences a 5% return on his outside investment, he will realize a gain of $1,250 over 12 months.

What is the common counsel of a financial advisor to a business owner? To invest more of his money *outside* of his business and chase higher rates of return. That's not the best advice.

So, let's look at what happens if this business owner were to invest the same $25,000, but earn a 7% annual return on his money instead of just 5% (which would take more risk). Here's what the end result would look like:

Annual Operating Expense	$1,000,000
Annual Outside Investment	$25,000
O.I. Rate of Return	7.00%
Annual O.I. Growth	$1,750

As you can see, the extra interest earned gained the business owner just $500 more.

Now, let's look at what happens if the same business owner focuses not on the money he is investing outside of his business, but instead he focuses on reducing areas of risk and loss. In the process, he identifies 1% of the expenses he was losing unnecessarily.

Reducing Expenses by just 1%	Saves in Dollars	Return equivalent on $25,000 invested	Which can be proven by the fact that:	Proof
1%	$10,000	40%	40% of $25,000 is:	$10,000

This example drives home the importance of focusing on maximizing the efficiency of a business's cash flow. If a business owner is able to identify and eliminate just 1% of expenses he was needlessly losing *inside* of his business, then that is a return equivalent to 40% of the $25,000 he was investing *outside* of his business!

There is more power in reducing unnecessary expense losses within a business than ever trying to pick the winners outside of the business.

Chasing higher returns takes risk. Reducing areas of risk and loss does not!

Reducing and eliminating unnecessary expenses and losses is good financial management!

I've had the opportunity to meet with countless business owners. The one recurring theme that I hear about is the need for access to capital. Many small business people are borrowing from and paying back someone else's bank each and every month, year in and year out.

- What if you had guaranteed access to capital to expand your business by 25-50% per year without ever calling a bank?

- What if you could accomplish this with the same dollars you are already borrowing and paying back to someone else's bank?

- What if only you determined when and how these loans were repaid?

- What if you could get back much of the cash you are spending within your business by eliminating unnecessary expense losses?

- What if you could get back the principal and interest payments your business currently pays to other financial institutions?

- What if your business had guaranteed access to increasing amounts of money to expand your business operations?

- What if you could build a substantial tax-free savings?

- What if I told you that you could accomplish all of this by simply being more efficient with the dollars you are already spending within your business?

You can! Just as savvy business owners do so each and every day by creating their own Personal Monetary System.

Using U.P.S. to Build Your Wealth

This chapter is where you will find some *Uncommon* Practical Strategies (U.P.S.) to Help You Build Wealth. These are not risky strategies, or hypotheses; these are proven strategies that have been used for decades by America's wealthiest families. The reason you aren't familiar with these strategies is because the government and Wall Street don't want you to know about them. They'd rather you gamble your money away in the stock market or qualified government plans so that *they* have access to *your* money.

So begin today to take back control of *your money* as you learn and apply these *Un*common Practical Strategies to help you build wealth.

How should you go about creating your own Personal Monetary System?

Establish a properly structured cash value life insurance policy (similar to a BOLI) through a mutually held dividend-paying Life Insurance Company.

Mutually held companies are some of the oldest financial institutions in the U.S. Many of these companies are between 100-150 years old. They have stood the test of time.

What is a mutually held company? Mutually held companies are accountable to their policyholders, not shareholders. They operate the same way as an electric co-op. Electric co-ops are owned by the people who use the power the co-op provides. Its customers are also its owners. A mutually held life insurance company functions in the exact same way. The policyholders are the ones who own the company.

A properly structured cash value (whole life) insurance policy is the ideal tool to create your Own Personal Monetary System. This concept was discovered in the 1980s by Nelson Nash, an Austrian economist and author of the best-selling book *Becoming Your Own Banker*. There simply is no other financial instrument that will allow you to access your money while allowing it to continue to employ the benefits of compounding interest.

The Value of CASH

The reason a cash value policy is so valuable as the foundation of your Personal Monetary System is that this vehicle enables you to build wealth long-term and benefit today by having CASH:

C – Compound Interest that Creates Wealth

A – Access to your Money Tax Free

S – Safe, Secure Investment with Guaranteed Returns

H – Heirs Receive an Inheritance Tax Free

Let's explore a real world example on the purchase of an automobile using your Personal Monetary System:

If you paid Cash:

If you were to pay cash for a car, say $25,000, you would save paying any interest, but the $25,000 would be gone, never to get it back. You would have avoided paying any interest to a bank. However, what could that $25,000 have earned you over the next 5, 10, 15 years or more? Lost opportunity cost is a real thing. This is why we say that you finance everything you buy. In fact, it can cost you as much by paying cash as it does to finance it through a bank. No one ever thinks this way. Again, you need to think and operate like a bank, or you will always be a customer of the bank!

Traditional Bank Financing:

If you were to finance a car through a traditional banking source, such as an auto finance company, not only do you pay all of the principal payments back to the bank, but you also pay them the interest. What do you have at the end of that five-year period? An automobile with a depreciated value. You certainly don't have the $25,000 in your possession, or any of the interest you paid the bank. That money is consumed and gone forever.

Financing your car with your own Personal Monetary System:

Now let's explore the exact same scenario utilizing a properly structured cash value policy. This simple process would consist of you opting to take advantage of the guaranteed loan option that the life insurance policy offers you as a policyholder. That's right, the loans are contractually guaranteed, which means you don't have to qualify to receive the loan. You can typically borrow over 90% of your current cash values in your policy, no questions asked.

Following the example above, you borrow the $25,000 from the life insurance company (instead of a bank). Where is your money? It's safely earning compounding interest while you use the life insurance company's money to buy your car.

Let's analyze the outcome of paying back this loan to the insurance company over a typical amortization period of 5 years or 60 months (just like paying a loan back to a bank).

What do you have at the end of these five years? You have your car just as you would have if you financed it anywhere else. The difference is that you also have regained access to the $25,000 cash value in your policy plus all of the interest and dividends that would have gone to the bank!

Note: The loan comes from the insurance company's general fund. You can borrow against the majority of the cash values you have in your policy (typically between 90%-95%). Your cash value serves as collateral for the loan should you not be able to pay the loan back. The cash value is guaranteed by the death benefit of your policy. As you pay back your loan, you are replenishing the amount of cash value your policy has available for you to borrow against in the future.

IMPORTANT: You must understand that your cash value never goes down. If you don't repay a loan, it does reduce the amount of cash that you have access to in the future. Remember, while you are using the insurance company's money, your total cash value continues to earn uninterrupted compounding interest. This is how Wealth Creators think and operate. It is very important that you use discipline to pay back your loan, just as if you had borrowed from a bank.

Do you see how this works? The insurance company is completely covered against loss. You get your car, plus you regain access to all of your cash value when you repay the loan.

You can now utilize those dollars (represented by the cash value in your policy) to repeat this process for another major purchase such as your next automobile or any other of life's major purchases that will demand some of your money.

These guaranteed loans also offer unstructured loan payment options. What does that mean? It means that as the policyholder, only YOU determine when and how loans are repaid. If there is an unexpected interruption in your household income, no one is going to call you if you don't make a payment for six months! How is this you may ask? It's because your death benefit is the collateral or guarantee for the loan. If for some reason you don't pay the loan back, the insurance company will proportionally reduce the death benefit paid to your beneficiary. You also don't have to worry about your credit scores being damaged. An important concept is that you want to pay these loans back just as if you had financed them at someone else's bank.

In addition to solving the equation of finance in your life, you can also utilize your life insurance policy to build a substantial tax-free source of income later in life. (Please note, in order to realize this benefit, the policy has to be setup properly by an experienced life insurance agent).

Borrowing against money you already have put away and can get to if necessary is less stressful than borrowing money you have yet to earn.

It's critical that you stop reading now and go to this website: *www.10MinuteLessonOnLifeInsurance.com.*

After you view the ten-minute lesson on Life Insurance, you will know more than 95% of agents out there, or at least what they are willing to tell you.

A properly structured policy will provide you:

1. Tax-Deferred Growth
2. Tax-Free Distribution
3. Competitive returns
4. High Contribution Limits
5. Collateral Opportunities
6. Principal That Is Never At Risk
7. Interest that is Guaranteed and Never at Risk

8. Guaranteed Loan Options
9. Unstructured Loan Payments
10. Liquidity, Use and Control of Your Money Today
11. And more....
   (See Figure 5)

Cash Value Life Insurance (CVLI) compared to other financial accumulation vehicles

	CVLI	HELOC	Margin	CD	Money Market	401 K
Tax Deferred Growth	Y	Y	N	N	N	Y
Tax FREE Distribution	Y	N	N	Y	Y	N
Competitive Return	Y	N	Y	N	N	Y
High Contributions	Y	N	Y	Y	Y	N
Additional Benefits	Y	N	N	N	N	N
Collateral Opportunities	Y	Y	Y	Y	Y	N
Safe Harbor	Y	N	N	Y	Y	N
No-Loss Provisions	Y	N	N	Y	Y	N
Guaranteed Loan Options	Y	N	Y	N	N	N
Unstructured Loan Payments	Y	N	N	N	N	N
Liquidity, use and Control	Y	N	Y	N	Y	N
Deductable Contributions	N	N	N	N	N	Y

Figure 5   Copyright 2013 Family Money Group, LLC

Look What the Wealthy Are Doing

It's worth noting that the IRS code which determines the taxation of Roth IRAs (Section 7702) is the same IRS code that governs a properly structured life insurance retirement plan. The big difference is that there are no income limitations on Cash Value Life Insurance plans (CVLI). Many high income earners are not eligible for Roth IRAs because they earn too much income. Additionally, contributions limits for CVLI plans are virtually unlimited in comparsion to the very limited ROTH IRA. This is one of many reasons why these policies are heavily favored by the wealthy. (See figure 5 on page 94)

Life Insurance is an "AND" Asset

A properly structured Cash Value Policy is unlike any other financial asset. Because of the unique benefits offered, life insurance is an "and" asset. In other words, you get the life insurance AND you get the real estate. You get the life insurance AND you own the gold and silver. You get the life insurance AND you have endless other opportunities to put those dollars to work for you, while never killing the miracle of compounding interest. One thing is for certain, when you have access to CASH, opportunity will seek you out! When you have access to CASH through your personal monetary system, you will discover opportunities that you never imagined. Contrast this to the common qualified plan where you are heavily penalized for accessing YOUR money.

The Banking Equation Solved

You should be in two professions throughout your lifetime. Your "day job" and banking. No matter what, banking will take place in your life. The big question is who controls the banking equation in your life? If you don't know the rules of the game, by default, the banks will happily fill this role in your life. By implementing a properly structured cash value policy, you have taken control of the banking equation in your life and it will have a dramatic impact on your financial future.

Living In The Real World!

Let's now explore a scenario involving two people who decide to save for retirement. We'll call them Fred and Ned. Both are 28 years of age at the time they begin saving for retirement. They both earn $85,000 per year. Both Fred and Ned save 10% of their income, which equals $8,500 per year. Fred decides to save with a common 401(k) plan and Ned opts to fund a high cash value life insurance contract.

In the real world do people lose their jobs? Ok, I think you know the answer to that. Of course they do. Now let us explore the outcome if both Fred and Ned lose their jobs at the end of the 10th year.

For the 401(k) returns, we will assume a recent 10 year snapshot of the S&P Total Return (2002 2013). You may be thinking to yourself, those were some bad years in the market! To this I would say, in the real world we don't get to choose when unfortunate events such as a job loss take place!

After both Fred and Ned lose their jobs, they both realize that they have a great business idea and opportunity. They each decide to tap their savings to fund their business

96

start-up as well as provide themselves the necessary cash to bridge the financial gap.

Remember Fred decided to contribute to his savings tax deferred. Fred has postponed all of his taxes. In this case, Fred postponed paying taxes on $118,216 till he lost his job and he needed access to his cash. Because Fred decided to save tax deferred, he did save approximately $44 per week in taxes over Ned. We are going to assume that Fred didn't take his tax savings and invest them. Most likely, that $44 a week in tax savings went to lifestyle consumption. I have personally seen this time and time again. This is what happens in real life.

Given his loss of job, Fred decides to take an early distribution of his 401(k). He requests his full $118,216 minus any taxes and penalties. Remember, Fred is not yet 59 ½, which means he has to pay the 10% penalty on top of his federal and state tax liability. We are going to assume Fred takes the standard deductions and exemptions available to him (approximately $11,773). This leaves Fred with a total tax bill of $31,090 plus the $11,821 early withdrawal penalty. This means Fred is now forced to pay $42,911! When it is all said and done, Fred's $118,216 ends being just $75,305 after he pays taxes and the penalty!

After Ned loses his job, he looks at his Cash Value Life Insurance policy and decides to request the maximum loan against his cash values, which equals $97,170. Since Ned incurs no tax bill or penalties, he has access to the full $97,170. In addition, since Ned is not using his money, but instead has taken a guaranteed loan from the insurance company, he continues to earn the full compounding interest and dividends on his entire savings!

It is important to understand that not all insurance companies are created equal when it comes to policy loans and the dividends paid to their policyholders. Some companies will reduce or eliminate any dividends proportional to any outstanding loans the policyholder has. This is called a direct- recognition insurance company. If the insurance company does not recognize a policy loan, then it is called a non-direct recognition company. This means that the insurance company pays the full guaranteed interest and any dividends regardless of whether or not there are any outstanding loans against the cash values.

For this example, I assume that Ned chose a non- direct recognition insurance company (for comparison purposes, I used an actual illustration and current dividend scale of a highly rated mutually-held life insurance company).

Study Figure 6 for a few moments. At the end of the day, Ned ends up with over $21,000 more money! Assuming there are no dividends ever paid (dividends are not guaranteed, however, most mutually-held companies have a track record of paying dividends consecutively for a century or more), Ned would still end up with more money than Fred. He also wouldn't have premium payments or loan payments.

By the 11th year, Ned's policy had enough guaranteed interest being credited that it covered his premium payments. Ned also continues to have peace of mind that he still has his permanent death benefit and continued growth of his cash values. If Ned's business is successful, he can pay back his loan and use those dollars again for retirement or possibly another loan to his business. This means he didn't kill the miracle of compounding interest!

98

Ned didn't lose out on any of the guaranteed growth or any dividends he would have received.

Unfortunately, the mainstream financial media, as well as a multitude of advisors, do not understand these strategies. Why? Because the masses have been conditioned to believe (remember Columbus and Galileo?) that the only way for Americans to save is to gamble by putting their money at risk.

401(k)	401(k) Totals	CVLI	Difference
Contributions over 10 years.	$85,000	$85,000	$0.00
Total Balance in beginning of year 11	$118,216	$103,493	$14,723
Total Deductions & Exemptions	$2,023 (Arkansas) $9,750 (Federal) =$11,773	N/A	N/A
Total Postponed Federal and State Tax Liability	$31,090	$0.00	$31,090
10% Early WD Penalty	$11,821	$0.00	$11,821
Total Taxes with Penalty	$42,911	$0.00	$42,911
Net Spendable Income	$75,305	$97,170	$21,865 more from Cash Value Life Insurance

Figure 6   Copyright 2013 Family Money Group, LLC

Contrast this to the insurance-based system of retirement which has been around for over 150 years, has survived every major financial depression, and has been helping the wealthy implement these uncommon strategies to build tax-free wealth generation after generation. The fact is that Wall Street cannot answer the following two questions affirmatively:

1. Can you guarantee the exact amount of money that I will have each and every month in retirement, and

2. Can you guarantee that I will not outlive my income? Any answer other than a "Yes", is an automatic "NO."

Life insurance is the only product that guarantees what you want to happen...will happen, even if you aren't around to see it happen!

Whose Future *Are* You Financing?

Yours...or the Government's and Wall Street's?

Mortgage Planning

As a Certified Mortgage Planning Specialist (CMPS), I counsel my clients on the importance of proper mortgage planning. Put simply, I show them how to:

Borrow Smart. Repay Smart.

I would define mortgage planning as: *strategically integrating your mortgage into your overall long- and short-term financial plan.*

Your mortgage is one of the most powerful financial tools that you have at your disposal. The way you go about managing your mortgage has far-reaching implications on virtually every area of your financial life, including your ability to save, plan for retirement, and pay for college.

Unfortunately the mortgage industry as a whole has been commoditized to the point where consumers narrowly focus on rates and fees. I witnessed this first hand during the 7 years that I actively originated mortgages.

Always Remember: A great rate on the wrong mortgage strategy can be a $300,000 mistake.

" We made the last payment and we were burning the mortgage to celebrate. "

Time to let go of the past...

It was commonplace in the early 1900s and throughout the great depression to have a clause in mortgages that gave banks the right to demand the full balance due on a mortgage. The banks could legally require someone to pay back the entire balance of the mortgage whenever they wanted their money, even if the mortgage holder was current and paying the loan on time.

When the stock market was flying high during the "Roaring Twenties," banks began gambling and speculating in the stock market. At the time, you could buy $10 worth of stock with only $1 of your own money and the other $9 was borrowed. Banks took advantage of this and began borrowing large amounts of money from each other. The banks regularly gambled this borrowed money in the stock market.

Their good fortunes didn't last long and the party came to a screeching halt on October 29th, 1929. Not only did the market crash, but over the next several years the market continued a consistent decline and ultimately it lost nearly 80% of its original value. Remember all that money the banks borrowed, gambled and lost? Well, all of those loans still had to be repaid! Where do you think they got the money to repay all these market losses?

They literally called up all of our parents and grandparents who had taken out a mortgage from the same banks that gambled their money away. The banks demanded they pay back their mortgages in full. As you can imagine, our ancestors didn't have the money to pay these banks back. The end result was that many people lost their homes.
102

Why did they lose their homes? It wasn't because our parents and grandparents gambled away their money. It was because the banks gambled their money in the stock market. Remember, at the time banks had the legal right to demand repayment of outstanding mortgage loans at any time.

Today, this is not the case. The rules have changed. Banks are restricted from borrowing heavily to gamble in the stock market. Banks are also prohibited from calling their mortgage loans due without cause. Today, there is only one reason you can lose your home to a bank, and that is if you stop making your mortgage payments.

Therefore, the only thing to really fear is not having the ability to make your payments. With that in mind, the main goal would be to have a lot of money saved up in an emergency fund in case you come across hard financial times.

"What is your rate?"

If this is the first question you ask when talking to a loan officer when buying or refinancing, or the only thing you focus on, then it could cost you.

For the majority of consumers, the most important part of finding the right mortgage is convincing themselves they have found the "lowest" interest rate. The fact is that a great rate on the wrong mortgage strategy can cost you hundreds of thousands of dollars over the life of the loan.

The lowest rate does not always save you the most money.

Let me give you one example.

I recently met with new clients who had just purchased a home. I showed them how they were paying $1,980 more per year, and how they had paid thousands more in mandatory loan program fees and upfront costs, which they could have easily avoided.

The original loan officer told them that he could get them a very low rate of 3.25% (which he did) with a specific loan program. What he didn't share with them (and what they didn't realize) is that if they had opted for a rate of around 4%, with a similar size down payment, they could have taken advantage of a different loan program where their payments would have been $165.00 *less* per month!

You are probably thinking that can't be right! Here is what was overlooked: The loan program they ended up with required a combination of upfront mortgage insurance premiums and monthly mortgage insurance premiums. The loan with the slightly higher rate had what is called lender paid mortgage insurance, which means the bank, not the borrower, would have paid these fees in an exchange for a higher rate.

What is your goal?

> To achieve the lowest rate? or

> To save the most money?

This is only one of many examples that I see regularly.

Managing your assets without managing your largest debt, is like heating and cooling your home with the windows wide open!

When I conduct a mortgage planning consultation, I take my clients through a very detailed loan comparison, which allows us to address these three very important questions:

1. **Does this make sense today?** In other words, what will it cost you today to get this loan? It is always a balance between cost and rate. The dirty little secret is, in order to get that "low" advertised rate, you will pay the bank substantial fees up front.

2. **Does this make sense from a monthly perspective?** What will your monthly payment of Principal, Interest, Taxes and Insurance (PITI) total? What is your effective percentage rate? (Your after tax rate).

3. **Lastly, does this make sense over time?** One of the most important questions you always want to ask yourself is how long you anticipate owning the property. If you plan to move within 10 years, it most likely does not make financial sense to pay up   front cost to achieve a lower rate because you won't be able to recuperate that money. You're better off opting for a slightly higher rate, which will actually save you money in the long run.

Many people assume that home equity is like cash in the bank. Before we dive into some mental snacks to chew on, it's important that you separate your house from your home.
(See Figure 7)

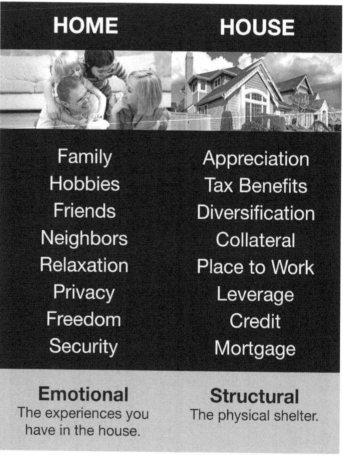

HOME	HOUSE
Family	Appreciation
Hobbies	Tax Benefits
Friends	Diversification
Neighbors	Collateral
Relaxation	Place to Work
Privacy	Leverage
Freedom	Credit
Security	Mortgage
Emotional	**Structural**
The experiences you have in the house.	The physical shelter.

Figure 7   Copyright 2013 Family Money Group, LLC

When it comes to managing the equity in your home, you should focus on your house. Notice that the items associated with the house focus solely on the financial aspects of the property. The home relates to the emotional experiences that are associated with owning the home. These are all great, but they should never be factored into how you manage the equity in your home. You must separate the two.

Understanding where the wealth transfers can occur in your mortgage can prevent unnecessary losses. I recently read a friend's Facebook post on the topic of paying one's mortgage off early. Here's what he said:

> "I've heard a lot of young people trying to pay down their mortgage ASAP. Typical advice is to only do this if you don't think you can earn interest higher than your mortgage rate on your investments. However, given the state of the markets right now... maybe we should all be paying down our mortgages."

I want to be very clear. I believe that everyone should pay off their mortgage as soon as possible. I define your mortgage being paid off when you have the money in your control to pay it off, not when you actually pay it off.

A key point to remember is that your house will go up or down in value regardless of your mortgage balance. You can store cash in your house, or outside of your house.

Have you ever considered what happens if you are in the process of paying down your house early the typical way, and God forbid, something bad happens? You may have just paid an extra $5,000 towards the principal with the goal of being mortgage free as soon as possible. Let's say you did this the month before you lose your job unexpectedly. Then what? You most likely can't access your cash unless you sell your house. This is neither a fast solution, nor a desirable one.

Remember, banks loan money against your income, not your house. If you lose your job (and thus your income) you won't qualify for a loan through a bank.

Think of the equity in your house from an investment perspective.

(Remember your house will go up and down in value, regardless of what you owe on your mortgage).

How appealing would an investment like this be to you?

- a minimum monthly contribution
- you can contribute extra money whenever you desire, however,
- if you need access to any of that money, you cannot easily access it.
- There is no guarantee of the value of your
- investment, and
- if you decide to contribute large sums into this investment, you still may see it go down in value.
- Even if you recently put an extra $5,000 into this "investment" you are still forced to contribute the minimum amount the next month.
- If for some reason you can't make the minimum monthly investment, you are at risk of losing all of your entire investment within 90 to 120 days!!

Is this a place where you'd like to invest your money?

Many people mistakenly assume that home equity is like cash in the bank. It's not! It's more like having money in a qualified plan like a 401(k) because it's very difficult to gain access to it even though it's your money.

If someone is rapidly paying off their mortgage and then a change in life happens, they would find themselves in a financial bind. At the moment you lose your job, or your income situation changes abruptly, it's little consolation that you only have 5 years left to pay on your mortgage. The bank won't care. In fact, they may be more likely to expedite the foreclosure process if you have substantial equity in your home. They want your next payment. If you can't produce it in short order, they'll foreclose on your house and you'll lose your home and all the money you've invested into the house.

Consider this example:

Jack:

· $300,000 - Home
· $100,000 - Mortgage
- $200,000 - Home Equity
- $0 - Emergency Reserve Account

Jane:
· $300,000 - Home
· $200,000 - Mortgage
- $100,000 - Home Equity
- $100,000 - Emergency Reserve Account

If you came across financial difficulties in today's economy, would you prefer to be in Jack's situation or Jane's?

Jane is obviously in a safer financial situation than Jack, even though she has a mortgage that is two times larger than Jack's mortgage!

Jack is in more danger of losing his home if he comes across financial difficulties or if the economy collapses. Jane has the cash to weather the storm while Jack is house rich and cash poor.

Remember, in hard times, you always want use and control of your money. Your home is a place to live in, not store cash!

Equity's Rate of Return

Some say that equity has no rate of return. In the strictest sense, this is true. This thought process comes from the fact that real estate values will go up or down regardless of the mortgage balance on the property. Therefore, if your home goes up in value, your investment of home equity did not cause it to do so. However, if you are accelerating the payoff of your mortgage the traditional way, you could say your return is the equivalent of your effective percentage rate or EPR.

What is your EPR? If you are currently paying 4% and you are in a marginal state and federal tax rate of 30%, then your EPR would be 2.8%. This is because mortgage interest provisions in the tax code allow you to deduct any interest paid on your mortgage. Therefore, once you factor in your hard earned dollars you keep instead of taxes you would have paid (had you not had a mortgage) your effective percentage rate is 2.8%. You might say that 2.8% is your return on the cash you are dumping into the home.

If you take this position and believe that home equity does have a rate of return, then you need to consider all of the facts. Over time, when you factor in the cost of home maintenance repairs, taxes, insurance and real estate commissions, your return, more often than not, is a negative one. This can easily be proven with math. This doesn't even take into consideration if the home actually goes down in value while you own it.

Are You Storing Money In Your Mattress?

" How much money does it hold ? "

We've all heard stories of people storing money in their mattress. As old fashioned as this idea may be, millions of people continue to use this practice today. Are you one of them?

Suppose you purchased your home 10 years ago for $150,000 and were able to sell it today for $215,000. That's a $65,000 increase. However, what many people fail to take into account is the cost of owning their house for this 10-year period.

Let's assume that you put $14,000 in improvements to this house over the 10 years that you owned it. In addition, it cost you $24,000 over this 10 year period in taxes and insurance. Lastly, most people end up enlisting a licensed real estate professional to help them sell their home. If we assume the typical 6% commission, this would equal

112

$12,900. Total all these up and you have paid in $50,900 over the 10 years that you owned this house. (See example at the top of next page)

If you sold your house, you would have the equivalent Compound Interest Return of: 0.68%! This return wouldn't even keep up with inflation, much less what returns you could get elsewhere. Remember, your house will go up and down in value regardless of what the mortgage balance is. The mortgage balance has NO effect on the value of your house when you sell it.

Before paying off your mortgage the traditional way (dumping cash directly into your house), you must take into consideration opportunity cost. If you are paying those extra dollars directly towards the principal on your mortgage, then yes it is true, you are no longer transferring the 2.8% (example on page 111) to the financial institution. However, you have failed to account for lost opportunity cost. What is opportunity cost?

Simply stated, if you pay $5,000 directly towards the principal of your house, you do save the 2.8% (example on page 103) you were transferring away; however, you also give up the ability to earn compounding interest on your money.

Current Market Value	$215,000
Original Purchase Price	$150,000
Improvements/Expenses (taxes, insurance, repairs, improvements & real estate sales commissions)	$50,900
Years Since House Purchase	10
Equivalent Compound Interest Return is: 0.68% You would have a gain of just $14,100 over 10 years. This is equivalent to an annual compound interest return of 0.68% over the same time period. How does this compare to inflation and your other investment returns?	

Your House is probably the largest personal investment you will ever make. How you decide to pay for it can create unnecessary wealth transfers, or it can create wealth. The choice is yours.

Building equity in your home by prepaying your mortgage is like storing money in your mattress. In fact, it may be worse because when your money is in your mattress you at least have access to it when you need it.

You need to make wise financial decisions if you're going to create wealth. Having "mattress money" may not be the wisest choice. The goal of paying off your mortgage can be accomplished more efficiently by using your Personal Monetary System. This way you'll not only have a paid-off house, you'll also have complete liquidity, use, and control of your money so that you can Finance Your Future and Retire Without Risk and leave a tax-free legacy to positively impact your family for generations to come.

Building a Third House

When you take out a mortgage, you build two houses: your house and the bank's house. If you aren't careful, you can end up building a third house —a house for the IRS.

Did you know that there are more tax deductions in the first 15 years of a 30-year mortgage than in an entire 15-year mortgage? Many people don't know that if they decide to pay a 30-year mortgage off in 15 years, they can save tens of thousands of dollars in taxes they would have paid had they chosen the 15-year mortgage.

A proper mortgage strategy not only allows you to pay off your mortgage early while maintaining liquidity, but it also allows the recapture of all the interest you are needlessly paying. It is true that by paying off your mortgage early you will save tens of thousands of dollars in interest. However, if you fail to understand the fundamental rules of money such as opportunity cost, then you will miss out on recapturing all of that interest you would have paid in a tax-free account that gives you complete liquidity, use and control of your money today.

The financial institutions don't teach you the rules. They're happy to "give you the clubs," but they're not about to teach you how to play the game to win.

If these strategies seem outside of the box and are shocking to you, that should be an indication that you've been listening to the wrong counsel.

Financing Your Next Vehicle

There are a number of methods you can use to finance a vehicle. Remember, you finance everything that you buy — whether you get a loan or pay cash. Here are the most common ways people finance their automobiles.

Lease: A very common strategy and one of the most inefficient ways to finance something. Leasing transfers more of your money to someone else (thus financing *their* future).

Bank Financing: The second most common (and inefficient) way to finance your car is through a traditional financial institution (bank). The way the typical American goes about financing a car, trading every 5 years, it not only costs the interest paid to the bank, but also the loss of the use of the money they are paying every month for that loan. It's a double loss!

116

What do you have at the end of that five-year period? An automobile with a depreciated value. You certainly don't have the $25,000 in your possession, or all the interest you paid. That money is consumed and gone forever.

And what does that bank do? They loan out your money to other people. So, not only is this costing the car buyer the interest they pay on that vehicle, but also what those interest payments *could* have earned them. How many vehicles will you purchase during your lifetime? Over a lifetime this can represent a major transfer of your wealth. It's the opportunity cost that you are giving up.

Let's assume that each automobile purchase is $30,000 and that you have the opportunity to earn 6.0% compounding interest over your lifetime. Let's also assume that you paid 6% to borrow the money each time. (Certainly the interest rate may be lower today, but 6% is closer to the historical cost of borrowing).

As you study the chart on the next page, you'll see that financing a vehicle not only costs you the interest that you paid to borrow the money, but what that money could have earned had you not transferred it away. The example below illustrates someone who finances a new vehicle every 5 years. Many households finance more than one automobile every 5 years. Over a lifetime, an individual can easily lose over $330,000!

The Reason Car Makers Like Financing! The Future Value of your interest paid compounded annually at 6%	
50 Years	$88,399
45 Years	$66,057
35 Years	$36,868
30 Years	$27,563
25 Years	$20,597
20 Years	$15,391
15 Years	$11,501
10 Years	$8,594
5 years	$6,422
TOTAL:	$330,773

Paying Cash:

If you were to pay cash for a car, you'd be out $30,000. It's true that you would save paying any interest, but the $30,000 would be gone, never to get back. Again you have avoided any interest to a bank. However, what could that $30,000 have earned you over the next 5, 10, 15 years or more? Lost opportunity cost is a real thing. This is why we say that you finance everything you buy. In fact, it can cost you as much paying cash as it does to finance it through a bank. No one ever thinks this way. Again, you need to think and operate like a bank, or you will always be a customer of the bank!

Using Your Own Personal Monetary System

Let's explore the exact same scenario utilizing a properly structured cash value policy.

This simple process would consist of you opting to take advantage of the guaranteed loan option the life insurance policy offers you as a policyholder. That's right, the loans are contractually guaranteed, which means you don't have to qualify to receive the loan. You can borrow against the cash value in your policy, no questions asked.

Following the example above, you borrow the $30,000 from the life insurance company (instead of a bank). Where is your money? It's safely earning compounding interest while you use the life insurance company's money to buy your car.

Let's analyze the outcome of paying this loan back to the insurance company over a typical 60-month amortization period (just like paying a loan back to a bank).

What do you have at the end of these five years? You have your car just as you would have if you financed it anywhere else. The difference is that you also have regained access to the $30,000 cash value in your policy plus all of the interest and dividends that would have gone to the bank!

Perhaps I should summarize it this way:

Remember the Debtor, the Saver and the Wealth Creator?

1. The **Debtor** will borrow money from a bank, because they have no savings. What is left after they pay off the loan? A depreciating asset (the car). Their money is gone forever.

2. The **Saver** pays cash for the car. They avoided paying any interest, but what are they left with? The same thing...a depreciating car. Their cash is gone forever. They never get it back!

3. What does the **Wealth Creator** end up with? They understand the power of compounding interest and using other people's money (OPM). After they pay back their own Personal Monetary System (their cash value policy), they will have (1) the car, (2) the original principal amount they paid for the car and (3) all of the interest that would have gone to the bank! Additionally, they receive any dividends paid to them instead of the banks' shareholders! They can now utilize this money again for future needs. There is no doubt which of these individuals has been most savvy with their money.

IMPORTANT: It's important to know that your cash values never go down as a result of taking advantage of a guaranteed loan from the insurance company. Remember, your cash values continue to earn uninterrupted compounding interest; thus you never "kill" the miracle. Your "collateral capacity" (the amount of your cash value that you can borrow against) does go down when you take a loan, but when you repay your loan (just as you would at a traditional bank) you are simultaneously restoring your collateral capacity. Following this process puts you in a position to borrow against your cash values continually for future major expenditures throughout your lifetime.

Paying for College

It's no secret that paying for college is a major hurdle for most families. The cost of a college education is skyrocketing. How you go about funding college is a major wealth transfer, one of those holes in your bucket so to speak.

The typical government plan, the way the government wants you to save for college, is through a government sponsored (there are those words again) 529 qualified plan. However, you pay a 10% penalty plus taxes if that money is not used for educational purposes. Again, you don't have use and control of the money.

And when you apply for grants and student loans, the federal government takes a dollar-for-dollar reduction in the amount of scholarships that you qualify for *because* you've been responsible and have saved in their government plan.

Compare this to how Wealth Creators pay for college…. They shield their college savings within their Personal Monetary System, which legally does not have to be disclosed. This way they can qualify for many more scholarships and grants and continue to have complete use and access to their money absolutely tax-free.

Let's also assume that your children don't need access to the funds within your Personal Monetary System because they qualify for scholarships. Guess what?? You get to use your money for whatever you want with no penalties and no taxes.

Just when the miracle of compounding interest is about to explode at the 18th year, what do most people do who followed the common strategy to take out a 529 qualified plan where the government wants us to save it? They transfer it away to the college's endowment fund for them to now put that money to work and take advantage of the miracle because we transferred it to them!

When you create your own Personal Monetary System, you have complete and total access to your money and can use it for whatever you want, whenever you want. So if your child wants to start a band and not go to college, you can help fund his band with no penalties and no taxes.

It's your money in your system
and the government doesn't tax it!

Your Guaranteed Retirement System

It's a fact: Insurance companies are sending income for life to millions of individuals around the country every month.

As I mentioned earlier, the legendary baseball player Babe Ruth, during the crash of 1929, when all his peers and many others lost everything and were wiped out financially, lived like a king during the Great Depression because he had all his money in a Guaranteed Retirement System.

Prior to the 1970s (and you probably know this from observing your own grandparents) people would receive a check in the mail every month. It was guaranteed to arrive every month and they never worried about it. Receiving a check in the mail was common before the 1970s. But then the government stepped in (with heavy influence from Wall Street) and established The Employment Retirement Income Securities Act. Wall Street saw the Guaranteed Retirement System as a threat and they needed to figure out how to get their hands on this money, so they heavily lobbied congress, which resulted in the ERSIA being passed. The culmination of their efforts came about in 1980 when they successfully got the introduction of the 401(k) which is, you guessed it, a government qualified plan. And today this is the most common retirement savings strategy used by most Americans.

During this same time, Wealth Creators avoided falling into this trap because they understood the power of having their own Guaranteed Retirement System, which provides them with:

1. Guaranteed income for life,

2. Long term care protection, and

3. Leaving a tax-free legacy to their children.

Establishing your own Guaranteed Retirement System is an *un*common strategy *un*known to most people. It's how Wealth Creators have amassed fortunes for decades.

Your Guaranteed Retirement System is *part of* your Personal Monetary System. You see, in order for you to Retire Without Risk, you need to begin controlling The Banking Equation by "plugging the holes" in your bucket so that you STOP transferring money to others and START Financing Your Future by using other people's money (OPM). This way you experience the "miracle" of compound interest that allows your money to grow uninterrupted and over time thus never "killing the miracle."

When you acquire the ability to "play the game" by using the right set of "clubs" you'll stop the banks, the government (as much as humanly possible), and Wall Street from gambling with your money and your future.

You work hard for your money. You need it to be there when you're ready to retire. And you should have complete control and access to your money during your lifetime. The only way for this to occur is for you to create your own Personal Monetary System.

Through these strategies, you will establish your own Guaranteed Retirement System and put yourself in position to achieve the 3 Retirement Goals most people have:

1. Guaranteed income for life,

2. Long term care protection, and

3. Leaving a tax-free legacy to their children.

When you begin working with a financial professional who can assist you in establishing your Personal Monetary System and Guaranteed Retirement System, you will have begun the journey of financing your future and Retirement Without Risk. It can be a challenging paradigm shift as you have been taught to believe something completely different (remember Columbus and Galileo), but what you'll soon come to realize (like Jimmy) is that *it's not too late for you to take control of your future* and stop gambling in the Wall Street Casino. It's time you begin to think and operate like a bank.

It's time for you to begin
Financing Your Future
so you can
Retire Without Risk.

David's Dictionary of Financial Terms

3 Types of Money
Every dollar you will ever have in your possession will flow to one of three places and ultimately become Accumulated, Lifestyle or Transferred Money.

Collateral Capacity
The amount of cash value in a properly structured whole life insurance policy that you can borrow against.

FDIC
The Federal Deposit Insurance Corporation. This is the entity that insures the deposits at a commercial bank should the bank become insolvent. Current deposits are insured up to $250,000 for each account. The FDIC, as of December of 2012, has less than 1 penny in their deposit insurance fund for every dollar that is deposited at the bank.

Federal Reserve (Fed)
The Federal Reserve is the central bank in the United States that has a monopoly on the creation of our nation's money supply. They have the power to create money with nothing of any intrinsic value backing it.

Fractional Reserve Banking System
Refers to the fact that commercial banks in The Federal Reserve System have the legal ability to loan out several times the money they have on deposit. Only a fraction of bank deposits are backed by actual cash-on-hand and are available for withdrawal.

Lost opportunity cost
What your dollar could have earned over a certain period of time had you not transferred it away to another party.

Major Capital Expenses
Anticipated and unanticipated expenses that will inevitably demand your money throughout your lifetime. Examples include—automobile purchases, new roof for your home, medical expenses, heating and air unit for your home, job loss, etc.

Market Correction
When "Securities" experience a drop in value, advisors who are big proponents of Wall Street will tell you not to worry and that "Corrections are a natural part of the stock market cycle." They'll say, "It always goes back up. It's time in the market, not trying to time the market." A stock market crash is said to be when stock prices plummet more than 10% in as little as one day.

Mega Banks (Too Big To Fail)
Banks whose owners and managers believe themselves to be exempt from the *processes* of bankruptcy.

OPM (Other People's Money)
Using money from another entity to make investments or purchases. This allows you to benefit from uninterrupted compounding interest of your own money, thereby maximizing the efficiency and growth of your money.

Open Market Operations
An open market operation (also known as OMO) is an activity by a central bank (The Federal Reserve in the U.S.) to buy or sell government bonds on the open market. The Federal Reserve uses them as the primary means of implementing monetary policy. A primary goal of open market operations is to manipulate the supply of money in an economy, and thus indirectly control the total money supply (through the banking system), in effect expanding or contracting the money supply.

Primary Dealer
A primary dealer is a firm that buys government securities directly from a government, with the intention of reselling them to others. Some governments sell their securities only to primary dealers; some sell them to others as well. Governments that use primary dealers include Canada, France, Italy, Spain, the United Kingdom, and the United States.

In the United States a primary dealer is a bank or securities broker-dealer that is permitted to trade directly with the Federal Reserve System ("the Fed"). Such firms are required to make bids or offers when the Fed conducts Open Market Operations, provide information to the Fed's open market trading desk, and to participate actively in U.S. Treasury securities auctions. They consult with both the U.S. Treasury and the Fed about funding the budget deficit and implementing monetary policy.

Qualified Plans
Retirement plans that meet the requirement of IRS code 401(a) and adhere to the Employee Retirement Income Security Act of 1974 (ERISA). Qualified Plans allow participants to deduct allowable contributions today in exchange for postponing the tax liability to an unknown taxation rate in the future.

Roth IRA
The Roth IRA allows individuals who fall under certain income thresholds to save for retirement with after tax dollars. Taxes are paid on contributions today in exchange, withdraws subject to certain rules are not taxed at all. These plans have very low annual contribution limits and higher incomes do not qualify to participate in these plans. Contributions to the Roth IRA are typically invested in mutual funds, stocks or other securities.

Securities
Wall Street's terminology to describe their products that offer no principal protection. In other words, they are products that have no guarantee you will get back what you put in.

Stock Market
The market in which shares are issued and traded either through exchanges or over-the-counter markets. Also known as the equity market. Owners of stocks have no guarantee that they will see a return of their principal.

Time value of money
The idea that money available at the present time is worth more than the same amount in the future due to its potential earning capacity. This core principle of finance holds that, provided money can earn interest, any amount of money is worth more the sooner it is received.

Money deposited today has the opportunity to earn interest. Because of this universal fact, we would prefer to receive money today rather than the same amount in the future.

For example, assuming a 5% interest rate, $100 invested today will be worth $105 in one year ($100 multiplied by 1.05). Conversely, $100 received one year from now is only worth $95.24 today ($100 divided by 1.05), assuming a 5% interest rate.

Wall Street
The collective name for the financial and investment community, which includes stock exchanges and large banks, brokerages, securities and underwriting firms.

Other Helpful Sites

www.RetireWithoutRisk.net
www.DLShowOnline.com
www.InfiniteFinancialServices.com
www.10MinuteLessonOnLifeInsurance.com
www.CMPSinstitute.org
www.InfiniteBanking.org

Recommended books and resources

Becoming Your Own Banker: Unlock The Infinite Banking
Concept by R. Nelson Nash

* *How Privatized Banking Really Works, Integrating Austrian
Economics With The Infinite Banking Concept*
by L. Carlos Lara and Robert P. Murphy, PHD.

What has Goverment Done to Our Money?
by Murray N. Rothbard

The Mystery of Banking by Murray N. Rothbard

*A History of Money and Banking in the United States, The
Colonial Era to World War II*, by Murray N. Rothbard

* *Borrow Smart, Retire Rich* by Todd K. Ballenger

* *The Creature from Jekyll Island* by G. Edward Griffin

* *The Great Wall Street Retirement Scam* by Rick Bueter

* The Wealthy Family by Chase Chandler

* *The Pirates of Manhattan, The Pirates of Manhattan II,
Highway to Serfdom* by Barry Dyke

The Mortgage Book, by Lee Welfel (Foreword by David Lukas)

Confessions Of A CPA, The Truth About Life Insurance,
by Bryan Bloom

*You can listen to me interview these authors on
www.DLShowOnline.com

About David

David is the founder and CEO at Infinite Financial Services in Little Rock, Arkansas. David's experience spans the Investment Banking, Mortgage Banking, Insurance, Financial Services and Real Estate Industries. David is a Certified Mortgage Planning Specialist as well as an Authorized Practitioner through the Infinite Banking Institute.

David has a successful radio show, which has aired for over 5 years. *The David Lukas Show* airs every Saturday in Central Arkansas on KARN 102.9FM and can be heard online at: www.DLShowOnline.com.

You can listen anytime with The Official David Lukas Show app which can be downloaded from the Apple® App Store, from The Amazon® App Store (Android^{TM}) and from the Windows® App Store.

Learn more about David by picking up the book by New York Times best selling author Robert Kiyosaki, *Rich Dad's Success Stories*.

David is committed to educating people on achieving financial freedom without risk. David and his team serve their valued clients all over the United States.

800-559-0933 | David@InfiniteFinancialServices.com

800-559-0933 | David@InfiniteFinancialServices.com

8900303R00084

Made in the USA
San Bernardino, CA
27 February 2014